P
He Was

"Misty Parenzan has written a book that will change the lives of women and their families. Her story is about a God who pursued her throughout her life, not because she was following Him and making 'right choices,' but because He had chosen her to be His before the foundation of the universe. To the person reading this book, this God who is Love also chose you. When I met Misty, a dear friend of my youngest daughter, I knew very little about her. However, our meeting was by divine destiny, and deep inside of me I knew that someday she was to write a book. You are holding that book in your hands.

Her words are not chosen to impress you, in fact there may be parts of this book she would have chosen to leave out, but her Heavenly Father has a plan, and He has gone before her to prepare the paths she is to walk. As she becomes more and more intimately acquainted with her Father, the more she discovers who she is created to be. Her identity is not defined by her past! Her loving heavenly Father gave her the Holy Spirit, who is her Teacher and Guide, and through Him, Misty discovered the Hidden Woman of the heart. The woman who was there from the beginning but needed to be discovered. She has chosen to believe that her identity is in The Source from which she came: God, her Father and Creator. Misty's story is the story for all women who place their identity in the things of the world – marriages, children, careers, ministry, possessions – these things will always leave us, in the end, empty. Our identity is found in one place and one place only, our Creator who loves us and redeemed us back to Himself."

—Germaine Griffin Copeland
President of the Prayers That Avail Much Ministries
(aka Word Ministries), and author of the
*Prayers That Avail Much* Book Series.

"Misty's open book nature bleeds through every chapter. Your heart will be touched and your faith ignited; mine sure was! It will be hard to put this one down, so carve out time for a full read."

—Jackie Vaggalis
Co-Pastor of Destiny Worship Center, Destin, Florida

"Misty's testimony is one of redemption and grace. In a culture filled with fear and despair, this story of hope and transformation can be the launching point for your personal realization that He was always there. The power in these pages is not only found in a story penned but in a life transformed. I have witnessed through Misty's life the power of His presence."

—Shannon Kanaday
Co-Pastor of Christ Chapel, Spring Hill, Tennessee

"What an honor and privilege to read and be a witness to Misty's incredible testimony! She writes with such vulnerability, authenticity and honesty. Once I started reading, I couldn't put the book down! This is a story of redemption and God's love for us! He doesn't promise we won't have hardships in this life, but He promises He will always be there!"

—AJ Strout
Founder of Goodness & Grit Entertainment
Franklin, Tennessee

"We all love redemption stories. And Misty's life teaches us what true restoration looks like. From despair to freedom, her powerful testimony will open your eyes to God's intentional, loving pursuit of each of us."

—Amy Groeschel
Co-Founder of Life.Church, Founder of Branch15
Edmond, Oklahoma

# He Was *Always* There.

# He Was *Always* There.

How a girl's life — clouded by trauma, addiction, and abuse — was restored by God's love.

MISTY PARENZAN

He Was Always There
Copyright © 2023 by Misty Parenzan

Paperback ISBN 979-8-9877230-2-9

All rights reserved, including the right of reproduction in whole or in part in any form.

Scripture quotations marked ESV are from The ESV® Bible (The Holy Bible, English Standard Version®), copyright © 2001 by Crossway, a publishing ministry of Good News Publishers. Used by permission. All rights reserved.

Scripture quotations marked NLT are taken from the New Living Translation, copyright © 1996, 2004, 2015 by Tyndale House Foundation. Used by permission of Tyndale House Publishers, Carol Stream, Illinois 60188. All rights reserved.

Scripture quotations marked NKJV are taken from the New King James Version®. Copyright © 1982 by Thomas Nelson. Used by permission. All rights reserved.

Scripture quotations marked TPT are from The Passion Translation®. Copyright © 2017, 2018, 2020 by Passion & Fire Ministries, Inc. Used by permission. All rights reserved. ThePassionTranslation.com.

Scripture quotations marked (NIV) are taken from the Holy Bible, New International Version®, NIV®. Copyright © 1973, 1978, 1984, 2011 by Biblica, Inc.™ Used by permission of Zondervan. All rights reserved worldwide. www.zondervan.com. The "NIV" and "New International Version" are trademarks registered in the United States Patent and Trademark Office by Biblica, Inc.™

Published in the United States by 9 Arrows Media

*To my beloved reader*

*As you read these God-stories, I pray your faith levels up. May His light shine through the words to heal what needs healed and mend what is broken.*

# Foreword

*"So if the Son sets you free, you will be free indeed."*
– John 8:36

The telling of one's story can be a powerful thing. Through telling, one can inspire change, teach principles, impart hope, and even create an environment for miracles to occur. Jesus used stories, or parables, to teach a generation about deeply spiritual topics but also to pave the way for them to actually receive and experience the supernatural Kingdom of God. In Revelation 12:11, the scripture tells us one of the ways to overcome the enemy of our soul is through sharing our testimony. A testimony is a story of triumph against impossible odds, covering the good, the bad and, yes, even the ugly parts of the journey.

In Hebrew, the word testimony comes from a root word which means, "to duplicate or repeat, to do it again." The telling of a testimony serves as an altar of remembrance for the teller, to remind the individual all that transpired to bring him or her to victory. But it also acts as a catalyst for additional miracles as the hearers are inspired that the breakthroughs spoken of in the story could also happen for them. With faith engaged, the triumph or miracle of the story is then repeated in the life of the hearer.

When I was a teenager, I was supernaturally healed of a torn cartilage in my left knee. I had been a state level gymnast and suffered a competition-ending injury and was scheduled for surgery. I was told that after surgery, I would never be able to compete again due to the extent of the damage. However, during the wait for the day of surgery, I attended a gathering of young believers who discovered my upcoming procedure. One of them said to me, "Well God made you; He can certainly heal you." Wow! This made sense to me! So they prayed for me, and I was instantly healed. My knee was suddenly stronger, and I could go up and down stairs without any further difficulty. However, my doctor was not a believer and insisted on still doing surgery, thinking I was just a religious fanatic with more zeal than sense. But was he ever surprised when he operated to find my knee was in pristine condition—no tears, no damage. Not only did God heal my knee, but I was also able to quickly rehab from the operation and competed once again only a couple of months later. Through the years, I have been able to share with others that Jesus really is a Healer. He made you; He can heal you! If He did it for me, He can do it again for you! This has sparked faith in others that has produced multiple similar miracles. This is the power of the story, the power of the testimony.

The book you hold in your hands is such a story. In *He Was Always There,* you will read the good, the bad, and the ugly of Misty's testimony; her journey through pain into purpose, from tragedy into triumph. You will laugh and you will cry. You will find the arms of a loving God who was not only always present, but preserved, forgave and embraced a broken life, and brought wholeness and peace against all natural odds.

Perhaps you will find small parts of your own story embedded along the way, or perhaps her testimony reminds you of someone else you have been praying for to receive freedom. Or perhaps her struggles look nothing like your own, but her life lessons learned will speak to your heart about not giving up, not giving in to defeat. This is a story of victory through every battle and of the rewards of persistently and consistently facing every challenge with God's help and the help of others.

In reading Misty's story, may your miracle be unlocked. Through her testimony, may you, too, find the faith and courage to overcome every challenge.

—Jane Hamon, Co-Pastor, Vision Church @ Christian International, Santa Rosa Beach, Florida, and author of *Dreams and Visions, The Deborah Company, The Cyrus Decree, Discernment* and *Declarations for Breakthrough*

## Acknowledgements

So many people contributed to the culmination of this project, and words alone can't express my gratitude, but I will try my best.

An enormous thank-you to all the people mentioned in this book as well as those not mentioned who have been a huge part of my life. Even though your name does not appear on a page, you are not forgotten in my heart. Thank you for your investment in my life.

Jane Hamon, thank you for believing in me and walking with me through this project. Your continued encouragement, guidance, feedback. and accountability kept me focused and on track. This book never would have been possible without you.

Rebecca Francis, your edits, questions, and suggestions made this book clearer, cleaner, and crisper without changing my voice.

Shelby McIntyre, thank you for making me do the ugly cry when I saw the cover. It exceeded my expectations by far. Your passion for creativity is evident in your contribution to this project.

My sweet girl Taylor, you are like a daughter to us. Thank you for all the times you stepped in to "hold down the fort" so I could focus on this project.

Dilan (baby #3), when you showed me your idea for my cover, my heart skipped a beat. Your script is my favorite. The sage flower couldn't be more perfect. Thank you for not being afraid to try.

Sage Yeatts, I believe it was for such a time as this that you were Dilan's roommate. Thank you for stepping in last-minute and bringing the art to life. I will be forever grateful.

To the rest of my kids, Travis, Bryana, Zoe, Saylor, Sage, Izzy, Asher, and Zane: I am honored the Lord chose me to be your mom. I grew up right alongside a few of you, which isn't always ideal, but I learned so much along the way. Thank you for loving me through my messes, forgiving and forgetting my shortcomings and embracing the me I am today. Y'all have been my biggest cheerleaders. I am eternally grateful!

To my best friend, companion, twin flame, aka hubby, Matt, your encouragement and support were such an integral part of this project. Thank you for always believing in me no matter what. We have come to know each other so deeply over the last couple decades. It's been both messy and beautiful at the same time. Loving someone well takes time, thought, and prayer. You've given all of these. I'm so thankful, and I can't imagine life without you.

Most importantly, I am thankful God lavishes His grace on my life and fills me with His spirit daily. May He continue to conform and transform me into His likeness and image through both the "burning bush" and His quiet whisper.

# Contents

| | |
|---|---|
| Preface | ix |
| 1 The Big News | 1 |
| 2 From the Beginning | 7 |
| 3 My Downward Spiral | 19 |
| 4 Motherhood | 31 |
| 5 My First Marriage | 35 |
| 6 Clearing the Slate | 45 |
| 7 New Beginnings | 55 |
| 8 The Year I Couldn't Hide | 65 |
| 9 Jesus Changes Everything | 73 |
| 10 Grace Upon Grace | 83 |
| 11 Our Greatest Loss | 87 |
| 12 Our Double Portion | 105 |
| 13 And the Journey Continues | 113 |
| Epilogue | 117 |
| 30 Days to a New You | 125 |

# Preface

*"Before I formed you in the womb I knew you, before you were born I set you apart. Do not be afraid for I am with you... declares the Lord."*
- Jeremiah 1: 5, 8 NIV

DECEMBER, 1976

I want to tell you about two couples, the first of whom wanted a child more than anything in the world. After almost ten years of marriage and several miscarriages, Ron and Wilma finally made it past the first trimester. They were elated. At about 30 weeks, some complications sent them to the hospital, where Wilma had an emergency c-section and a hysterectomy. Their baby girl did not survive. This couple returned home devastated, hopeless, and hysterical.

In contrast was a couple not far away. They were 16, unmarried, and expecting a baby. The mother didn't know she was pregnant until well into her pregnancy because of her alcohol and drug use. She feared the responsibilities that came along with raising a baby. In her seventh month of pregnancy, she went into early labor and gave birth to a baby girl, who weighed just under five pounds. Fortunately, the baby was healthy. This couple had no idea what they were going to do. The mother knew she couldn't give this child the life she hoped for. Coincidentally, their close friend's mother knew a couple who had just lost a baby. Within a day, the new 16-year-old mother had made one of the hardest, most selfless decisions she would ever have to make: to let her daughter go.

A few days after Wilma returned home, she received the call from her best friend that a young mother, whom her son knew, wanted to give her baby girl up for adoption. Wilma was overjoyed. She hung up the phone and quickly packed a bag to head back to the hospital. At first, her husband and family, who had been consoling her those past few days, thought she was having a nervous breakdown when she announced she was going to the hospital to get her baby. After some explaining, they loaded up and headed to the hospital to see their new baby girl.

This baby girl was me.

The first time I was told I would write a book was in February 2008 at a women's conference. The speaker, Germaine Copeland, called me out during the service and said one day my story would be in a book. I remember thinking she obviously didn't know me. Writing has never been my thing. I love math and logic. Math is absolute, and it always has one answer. I never enjoyed writing as a child either. It uses pieces of my brain that don't come naturally. I also lacked time. Every week since then, someone has asked if I've ever thought of writing a book or told me I need to. Most mornings, I'd ask the Lord who it was going to be, and He never disappointed. I told Him years ago to bring me a ghostwriter, so I could tell all my stories, and boom, the book would be written... I never found one. Here I sit now, finally ready to share.

I filled this book with stories from my life, where it all began and where I am today. God is full of redemption, grace, and mercy. We all have God-stories, and if we pay attention, we can see Him everywhere. I am always looking for what He's doing. There are no coincidences in my life. These stories bring hope to the lost and broken and their loved ones, which includes everyone. No one is ever too far gone for the Lord. I was almost 30 before I let Him transform me. I pray that as you read these stories, it will inspire you to change your life. Give God a chance. Jesus Christ can and will rescue you no matter what. You are worth it. He has quite the sense of humor, so be ready! One thing I know for sure...

He was always there.

# 1
## The Big News

FEBRUARY 1997

As we pulled into the driveway that sunny afternoon in February, the last thing I expected to see was my parents' car parked in front of my house and them standing at the front door. For most people, this may be a normal situation, but for me, it was unsettling. My parents had never stopped by unexpectedly. We didn't have that kind of relationship. They knew I didn't like them to show up unannounced. They came over either for dinner or to babysit, but we always planned it.

The Phoenix valley in February meant cool sunny days perfect for being outside. Nick, my husband of almost a year, and our six-month-old son Travis, had spent that afternoon at the park. We sat in the driveway for what felt like hours, thinking of all the explanations for my parents' visit. I had a sick feeling in my gut. Neither one of us wanted to get out of the car, but we had no other options. As we approached them, I noticed a large manila envelope in my mom's hand. They didn't give their usual over-the-top greeting to Travis but were rather serious instead. I casually asked what was up and what was in the envelope, without showing how bothered I was about them being there. My mom said she had something very important to talk to us about. My dad was quiet as usual. We stood at the front door in an awkward silence, waiting for Nick to unlock the door. Once inside, we walked in and headed to the family room. With Travis amongst his toys, I sat on the floor impatiently waiting for them to talk. Nick got something to drink in the kitchen as they sat on the couch, still holding the manila envelope. I again asked what was in the envelope. My mom started babbling on about how she had something very important to tell me, that she never intended for me to know, but there were circumstances arising that led them to believe I would soon find out from someone else. She tossed the envelope to me on the floor and said, "Well, it's all there."

As I pulled the papers out, I noticed they were court papers of some sort. I read about a baby girl born on December 14, 1976 (my birthday), to her mother, Gayle Houser, whom Ron and Wilma Hastings adopted. The rest of the packet became a blur. I sat there on the floor thinking there was no way these two people waited twenty years to tell me they adopted me. My inability to connect with my parents over the years, and all the feelings that I didn't belong, came flooding back. Instantly, I had the answer to the constant questions while growing up about why I didn't look like my parents. The only health history I ever knew, which was absolutely horrible, was all void. I wanted to know who else knew about this, and if she was ever really pregnant. I questioned everything they had ever told me. I just sat there and stared at the papers. I was in complete shock. I was angry... but sadly, I was more relieved than anything. The many fears that I had that were based on the lie that these two people were my biological parents were no longer valid. I could've avoided many things in the previous few years had I known this information.

My mom began crying and rambling about how great it is being my mom, that she would always love me, and that no matter what I did, she would always be there for me. She continued her "crazy talk," while I just sat there. My dad stayed quiet—didn't say one word. Her thinking that her time as my mom was over made me even more angry. She had no idea what keeping this secret had done to me. I had felt lost and alone most of my life. I always felt like something was missing and spent countless moments searching for that thing, coming up empty-handed every time.

She told me she was seven-months pregnant with a baby girl in December 1976, but after some complications, she had an emergency c-section and hysterectomy. Two days after coming home from the hospital, her good friend, also named Gale, who later became my godmother and gave me my middle name, told her of a baby girl whose parents decided not to keep her. That's when my parents jumped in the car and headed to Iowa City to adopt me. The only people who knew were a few of their siblings who were with them during that time and were all sworn to secrecy.

When she asked if I was interested in finding my birth mom, I quickly responded "yes." She knew someone who might know Gayle's whereabouts. Although my godmother was no longer alive, my mom had her son's number, who was friends with my birth parents all those years ago. I still hadn't moved from my seat on the floor. I just sat there staring at the piece of paper with the phone number on it. My parents stooped down to hug me, but I just gave them a little pat. I was glad they were leaving. Nick hadn't said a word the entire time, either. The air in the room felt thick.

After they left, I immediately dialed the number. Startled that he answered, I asked him if he knew a Gayle Houser. He got quiet and seemed hesitant to give me any information, so I told him my name, that I was born 20 years ago, and that I was pretty sure Gayle was my birth mom. He couldn't believe I actually called. He told me Gayle had been looking for me all these years, and she would be excited to hear from me. Rather than give me her information, he took mine and said she would call me soon. After the call ended, I sat there repeating the words, "I am adopted. I am adopted. I am adopted."

## HE WAS ALWAYS THERE...

That day rocked my world; however, now that I am healed, I can see God's hands all over my adoption. My parents never planned on telling me. A cousin who went against the grain and made a family history book, which noted my adoption, forced my parents' hand. That was God. That it only took me three days to connect with my birth mom, on her birthday and my anniversary, was also God. It is no coincidence that my middle name, although spelled differently, is the same as my birth mom's. Gayle even remembers how easy it was to find a family to adopt me. All the pieces had to align, and when that happens, I recognize His hand and give God the credit.

Can you think of a time in your life when all the pieces lined up perfectly? Some people call this luck, but there is no such thing as luck. The Lord moves in our lives, whether or not we know Him. It's up to us to open our eyes and look around.

## 2
## From the Beginning

I didn't have a terrible childhood, but I didn't have a great one either. Looking back, I can say my parents did the best they could with what they had. Losing a baby a few days before adopting me probably didn't set a great stage. Keeping it all a secret was even harder. They were both raised in big families in the rural parts of Illinois, with little money during what was called the silent generation: a period of war and economic depression in which they experienced hardships of the Great Depression and World War Two. They grew what they ate and made what they wore. Neither of them had simple conveniences growing up, like indoor plumbing or running water. My dad served his time in the military and was a quiet man. They married in their mid-twenties, and my mom "wore the pants" as they call it. They fought hard for ten years to have a baby and experienced loss after loss until they were left with only one option.

I was born in Iowa, where I spent the first six years of my life. Those years are filled with memories of large gatherings of extended family. By the time I came along, my parents were in their late 30s. Their siblings had been having babies for decades, so I had lots of first and second cousins to play with, which was great because I was an only child. My dad's mom was the only grandma I remember, and she was my favorite. We spent many weekends at her house. She lived in a small town with a population of less than 300. This is where my dad grew up. She was just getting running water and indoor plumbing when I was around four years old. I remember using the stinky outhouse and getting water from the well. To take baths, we boiled water on the stove and shared the same tub of water with others. My grandma loved Jesus and was the first one to tell me about Him. She taught me the song, "Jesus Loves Me." As an adult now, I know she was a praying woman. Unfortunately, we moved to Arizona when I was six, so my visits with her were only during the summers until she passed away when I was ten.

Being an only child, I was spoiled. Times were tough for my parents in the early '80s, although I never knew it because I always had the latest and greatest toy. The factory my dad worked at closed down, and he was without a job for quite some time. They had a friend who told them of an opportunity in Phoenix, Arizona. So in 1982, our family of three moved thousands of miles away from all my extended family. I was sad to be leaving Iowa and everything I ever knew to be home. There would be no more family gatherings or time with my grandma.

We moved a lot during our first few years in Phoenix. My mom's sister eventually followed us to Arizona with her daughter and two grandsons, who lived with us off and on. One day, my cousin left her older son, who was my age, with us and didn't return until the following year. As a child, I didn't realize how sad this must've been for him, but as an adult looking back, it breaks my heart. That year, the two of us made a lot of bad choices. We stole things from the local Circle K just because we were bored. We snuck wine coolers out of the fridge and spoke swear words to be cool. We also played games we shouldn't have. No one gave us proper direction or guidance. Church was never part of our lives. My parents both worked full time, and we went to a sitter's house each afternoon with a bunch of other kids who had zero direction as well. At the end of that school year, his mom came and picked him up and dropped off his little brother for the summer. It's no wonder these two boys struggled in their adult years.

Summers were my favorite. Since my parents both worked, I would spend half the time in Illinois visiting all my favorite family members, hopping from house to house, going to county fairs, attending family reunions, visiting my grandma, and reconnecting with old friends. I'm not sure if I loved it because I was there without my parents, or if I just loved all the cousins to play with. The other half of the summer, I would be with my cousins who lived close to us. We had very little parental supervision, so we did whatever we wanted. We watched rated-R movies, stole things from stores, played truth or dare with their friends, and roamed the neighborhood. No one in my life modeled moral character.

When I was ten, I had a dream that rocked my world. In the dream, my grandma had come to me and told me her time on earth was over, but she had a very special picture that was just for me. She told me where it would be, so my dad could get it when he went there for her funeral. I woke up shaken. That very evening, my parents came into my room and told me she had passed. I couldn't believe it. I told my dad about the dream, and he thought I was making it up, but I made him promise he would look in the side drawer of her bedside table for the picture. The picture was of Jesus. I later convinced myself that I made the whole thing up because it was just so shocking.

I ruled our home. Whatever I wanted, I got, leaving me to always want more. I can't remember a time in my childhood when I felt happy or satisfied. Most of the time, I felt empty, alone, misunderstood, and different. It made little sense to me because I excelled in most things I attempted. I was a straight-A student, I played multiple instruments, and I loved to sing. In my parents' eyes, I could do no wrong. I had the master bedroom in my house. They often praised me and told me how proud they were of me, but other times, my mom accused me of loving friends and other family members more than her. She would yell at me for my disrespect and lack of communication with her. She would throw things at me, saying all she ever wanted was a daughter who loved her. I never understood why I didn't give my mom the respect or love and attention she wanted. I just thought I was an ungrateful brat, and no matter how hard I tried, once I was in her presence, any chance of success was gone.

I was much closer to my dad. He eventually learned to stay out of our arguments because my mom would accuse him of taking my side, saying nobody loved her, so she might as well die. My dad and I had an unspoken understanding that although he didn't agree with her, it was just best he stayed out of it. The day following her blowups, she would take me shopping with her and buy me things. That was her way of apologizing, but then she would yell at me for being unappreciative because my attitude didn't change as she wanted it to. No one outside of our home saw the side of her my dad and I did.

By 12 years old, although I still appeared to be a good girl, I was a mess. I had a nasty mouth, stole from stores while never getting caught, and was rarely honest with my parents about anything. My path would destroy me if I kept going. As a latchkey-kid of the '80s, I spent most afternoons at home alone playing video games, listening to music, or watching TV. I spent most evenings roaming the bowling alley or bingo hall while my parents played. That was where I learned what adults were like. I thought all adults used swear words, drank alcohol, and stretched the truth because that was all I saw. Those things were like driving—something people get to do when they are older. Sadly, I still had no friends who influenced me positively.

In sixth grade, I was assigned a partner to do a research paper with. Her name was Allison, and although we'd been in school together since third grade, we never connected until then. Her mom, who later became like a second mom to me, was always the room mom and was at school all the time. I vowed in my heart that I wanted to be a mom like that one day.

Allison was good for me. The first time I took the Lord's name in vain in front of her, she immediately called me out and told me how bad that was. When I said a swear word, she told me about that as well. I loved going to her house. She had three sisters, and her house was always filled with life, laughter, sibling fights, and so much love. Their family dinners were my favorite. The atmosphere in her home was completely opposite of mine, and I craved it.

It wasn't long before Allison invited me to her youth group one Wednesday night, which happened to be at the Mormon church across the street from my house. That first night was so fun. I hadn't realized how many kids from school went there. Suddenly, I had lots of new friends. The group leaders were kind and accepting. After a few Wednesdays, I tried out a Sunday. I began attending as many things as I could. I started reading the Bible and The Book of Mormon and surrounding myself with families and friends from church, but I still didn't feel like I belonged there, either. I was the only one whose family wasn't part of the church. However, I still felt different or out of place. I felt alone and misunderstood and believed people didn't know the real me.

I loved everything about church. I learned morals and how to serve, and I built many good relationships. I begged my parents to let me get baptized for years, but my mom hated church. She didn't like me having fun with the other moms. She was jealous of me always wanting to be there. I kept asking though, and when I turned 15, she gave in. I was so excited to be a member and not just the girl who came without her parents. Shortly after, my mom attended with me, and things changed. She would be one way at church and another at home, losing her temper with me. If I said anything about it, I would get in trouble. I hated the pretense. Her hypocrisy pushed me further away, and I eventually quit going to church altogether.

Home life got rockier. My parents screamed and fought daily, throwing dishes and breaking things. They would talk about divorce, and I would say I would only live with my dad. My mom would call my friend's parents and ask what I said about her while I was there. Of course, they were confused because I never said anything about her. As a child, I didn't even know how to put into words the craziness that surrounded her or the severe effect her mental state had on me. The verbal abuse caused me to put up walls around my heart that no words could penetrate.

High school came with its own set of challenges. School always came easily for me, and teachers always loved me. At the start of ninth grade, I was attending church regularly as well as an early morning class that Mormons take, called seminary, before school each morning, and I was active in my youth group. My closest friends were from church. They convinced me to run cross country with them. Someone told me that running helps you lose weight, so I was all in. We had practice five days a week at 6:00 AM and 6:00 PM for the first four weeks. Getting in shape was tough. It was my first experience with exercise. I started learning about nutrition and what eating right looked like. I grew up on TV dinners, hamburger helper, and pot pies. I was always on the chunky side, which we now call curvy. I hated that I could never trade clothes with my friends because they were all so skinny. One of my deepest desires was to be thinner and prettier, which I now know were all lies from the enemy.

Over the next few months, my body started changing. I experienced what is now called a "glow up." I lost about 20 pounds, got my braces off, and learned how to do my hair and makeup. Suddenly, boys talked to me. The attention was foreign to me, but I liked it. One rule of thumb that Mormons stand by is to limit friendships with and never date non-Mormons to avoid getting into trouble. I didn't see the value of this rule until it was too late. Since my parents weren't Mormon, they didn't know about it; therefore, they didn't enforce it. This is where my trouble started. Sadly, I didn't realize that my church friends were the real deal. But I found that I felt more comfortable with the unchurched kids. I began going to parties rather than youth group. I skipped seminary and church on Sundays to sleep in. My church friends would reach out, but I avoided them for fear of their judgment.

In the spring, a friend asked me if I would help her do the stats for the boy's baseball team. I had no idea what that meant, but it sounded fun. It was not a good environment for me at all. We spent our afternoons in the dugout and rode long bus rides weekly with all the baseball players—unwise.

A couple weeks in, a really good-looking senior asked me out. I couldn't believe a senior wanted to take me out. I was so excited… but so naive. My parents didn't object. They said yes to anything, not thinking of repercussions. We planned for him to pick me up, grab take out, and watch a movie at his house. When I realized his parents were out of town, I told myself it was no big deal. He wouldn't try anything on our first date, right? Wrong! Minutes into the movie, he kissed me, and I thought, "Wow. He must like me." Then he touched me in places I'd never been touched before. I felt uncomfortable. I didn't know what to do. Before I could respond, we were on his hard carpeted floor, and he had my pants down. I told him I had never done this, and I wasn't ready. He just said to trust him, and I would like it. The pain I felt when he entered me was like no other. I couldn't stop him. What probably only lasted 30 seconds felt like hours. No matter how many times I asked him to stop, he kept at it. When it was finally over, he stood up, put back on his pants, and asked if I was ready to go home. I didn't say another word. The two-mile drive felt like ten. As soon as I got home, I jumped in the shower and cried. I was no longer a virgin. I felt dirty, rejected, used, and stupid. What was I thinking? I blamed myself.

The next day at the game, he didn't even acknowledge me. I was so afraid to tell anyone for fear of him denying it. I was filled with shame and regret. The rejection from that incident cut deep. My self-image and self-confidence suffered tremendously. My only choice was to suck it up and move on as if nothing ever happened.

I spent the final months of my freshman year getting drunk at parties and making out with guys, though never as far as sexual intercourse. I had no desire to ever experience that again. But I learned all about oral sex and engaged in that. Alcohol made it easy and fun, until it didn't. I got so sick at one end-of-year party that I passed out and woke up in my own vomit. The humiliation from that night motivated me to never drink like that at a party again. I was thankful the year was over.

My time in Illinois that summer was a bit different than my other visits. I was no longer a little girl. I had changed drastically from my last visit. All the attention was exciting. Boys noticed me and asked to take me out. It filled deep places in my soul. I knew my dad loved me, but he was never good with words. I always looked elsewhere to find my value. At the start of my sophomore year, my dad had a stroke that brought him home permanently. Probably the works of God himself. Up to that point, I had come home to an empty house every afternoon, but from then on, my dad was always home. I am sure it kept me out of a little trouble.

That year I started dating a guy named Ryan. He was a baseball player, and we had most of our classes together. We became a typical high-school couple. We spent every moment together, mostly at his house because we could be in his room with the door shut. I finally gave in the following year to having sex. I was terrified from my first experience, but I couldn't keep saying no. Thankfully, it was nothing like that first time. Our junior year flew by. We talked about life after high-school, college, marriage, kids. We were young and clueless, but I believe our relationship kept me out of trouble during that time.

I attended church every now and then but hated how guilty it made me feel. I missed those friendships that used to warm my soul. I missed the big family dinners and the youth events, but I had convinced myself I was a bad influence, and they were better off without me. I wasn't like them, anyway. I crossed lines they'd never even approach. With only one year left of school, I was impatient to move into adulthood. I had no idea what that next year had in store for me.

HE WAS ALWAYS THERE...

Looking back at my childhood through healed eyes, I can see God's hand present throughout. I know He gave me the dream the night before my grandma passed. He also brought the right people at the right times, but unfortunately, so did the enemy. The devil's voice was louder at the time, and because I had no understanding of my true identity, that's the one I followed. While the Mormon church taught me morals and values, they did not teach me about Jesus being a Savior who loved me and had a higher purpose for my life. It was just religion to me instead of a relationship with God, so my heart never changed. Ultimately, my time there was never about knowing who God was to me, but rather just about the friendships I had when I went. I still carried a deep emptiness inside; however, looking back, I can see His hand drawing me, wooing me, nearer to Him... I just didn't know it then.

Can you think of a time in your childhood when you look back with a sense of regret, knowing you missed the call of God or the windows of opportunity He gave to draw near to Him? Have you forgiven yourself for listening to the voice of the enemy instead of hearing the voice of God, and for any bad choices that resulted from that? Even now, He is standing with open arms to love you and heal you from the childhood wounds that shaped your early life. Tell Him all about it, and receive His forgiveness, healing, and love.

# 3
## My Downward Spiral

*"There are some of your graces which would never be discovered if it were not for your trials."*
– Charles Spurgeon

My life changed the most the year I turned 18. I had learned to live with family dysfunction. Still living at home, I was a good student, a hard worker, and drug-free. But all that changed in a year marked by one trauma after another.

I turned 18 in December, 1994, my senior year in high school. My birthday excited me because it meant I could finally get a job and make my own money. Until that time, I hadn't had a real job. My parents wanted me to focus solely on school, but that meant depending on them for money. When I wasn't at school, I was at my boyfriend Ryan's house. We'd been together since our sophomore year, so we were serious. We had been sexually active for almost two years and talked of marriage often, which baffles me now.

I was excited to be old enough to take a class to become a Certified Nursing Assistant (CNA) at a local nursing home. It was two 40-hour weeks of class, and there was one over Christmas break. I wanted to be a nurse. I had spent the two previous summers taking community college classes to get a head start. Goal-oriented, I was in the top 1% of my high school class. I had already earned a full scholarship to any in-state university and a partial scholarship for out-of-state ones. School came easily for me. I wanted to be a CNA because the local nursing home had a position where I could work 36 hours on the weekend and get paid for 40 hours. It was a great setup. The pay was amazing, and I felt it was a step toward my goal.

That January, I was no longer home on the weekends. I loved the new freedoms that came with this job. I met new people who weren't really the best for me, but I didn't know it. Even though I was 18, the people I spent time with were in their 20s and 30s. Many shifts ended with an invitation to get high or drink. Sometimes I would join them but not participate. I spent less and less time with Ryan, and more and more time with an older crowd, unaware of how unwise these choices were.

A guy named Randy caught my eye a bit, and I caught his. He was 20 and didn't do drugs like the others, so he and I were the only sober ones. He had just won a free trip to Disneyland in April from a radio contest and was looking for a friend to bring. I couldn't believe he asked me. I remember thinking he was just caught up in the moment; there had to be someone else he'd rather take. After all, we had just started talking that night, and I was only 18. I had to say no. I had a boyfriend, school, and work, but I loved that he asked me.

Life at home went from bad to worse. My parents obsessed about my grades even though they were still the same. Their worry came in threats: if your grades drop, or if you don't get up for school, we will take your car away. It bothered me because I hadn't given them any reason to worry. My grades were still top-notch, and I always got up for school. I spent most afternoons with Ryan or friends from work, then home by bedtime, just to get up and do it again. My relationship with my parents was strained. I had freedom to do anything, but they tried to control with empty threats, and they were really clueless about the issues I faced. My mom had been mentally unstable my entire life. She was insecure and always wanted to know my feelings, which I didn't know how to express for myself. We fought all the time!

In March, I took a trip to visit family and friends. I needed a break from school, work, and my boyfriend. But this trip began my downward spiral.

On my first morning at my friend's house, as I was getting ready for the day, her husband came into the bathroom behind me. He remarked how happy he was that I was 18 years old, so he could finally have a piece of me. He was a joker, so I laughed it off and tried not to react. Then he put his arms around me and asked if I'd ever been with a real man. I tried to play it cool until I realized he was serious. My heart stopped, and my stomach turned. I had been spending summers at his house for the past ten years, playing with his kids, attending county fairs, sharing meals. When I told him I wasn't interested, he promised I wouldn't regret it, and he would give me the best time. I asked him about his wife, and he told me of course he loved her, but there was nothing wrong with having fun. He also said if I refused, he would tell his wife that I made a pass at him, and it would be my word against his. So I laid on the bed and let him have his way.

It took me over ten years to realize the trauma from that event. The "me" today would've never let this happen. But I was a young, naive 18 year old, who was forever changed by this moment. I was so full of shame, guilt, and anger for allowing this to happen. I questioned why I didn't stop it. I felt dirty, and it scorched my view of the sanctity of marriage. I couldn't stop rehearsing a different outcome in my mind. I packed up and left that day. I didn't even say hi to the kids. The rest of that trip is a blur. I can't even remember how I got back to Arizona. What trauma can do is crazy. Trauma fragments the soul and causes negative things, just like sin and generational curses do.

The night before school started back after my spring break trip, which ended in trauma, my mom was threatening me that my grades better not drop the last semester, and if they do, then no car, no friends, no working... on and on. Hearing her threats for no reason exasperated me so much, I threw out my own threat. I said if she kept at it, I would hand my backpack over, not return to school, and move out. I was 18, and I believed I had that right. She obviously thought I was bluffing because she had to get the final word. She said, "well, like I said, if those grades drop..." I went to my room, grabbed my backpack and put it at her feet, and said "thank you." I packed up some things, called a friend, and walked out the front door.

My parents tried to stop me, but there was no stopping me. I had a nice chunk of money saved from the three months of working all those hours, so I wasn't worried.

I headed to a co-workers house because I didn't know where else to go. After listening to my story, she asked me if I wanted to get high with her. I had never tried marijuana before this day, so I thought, "Why not?" Her 20-year-old friend, Randy, was hanging out with her when I got there, and he wanted to move out of his house, too. He was also an only child and was having trouble at home. The next morning, he and I went looking for an apartment. We found a two-bedroom in our price range, signed on it that day, and moved in a few days later. He asked me again if I wanted to join him on his Disney trip at the end of April. That was an easy yes. Things seemed to fall into place.

When I went to my parents' to get my things, my mom was in hysterics. She insisted on helping me move for fear of not knowing where I was going. My parents knew I wasn't changing my mind. I packed all my things and wrote a letter to Ryan, telling him it was over. I don't remember what I wrote, but I am sure it rocked his world. I ignored many calls from the school and friends. Looking back, I had no idea how much the trauma of my spring break trip affected me. In just weeks, I left my home, quit school, broke up with my long-time boyfriend, tried drugs for the first time, moved in with another guy and cut off all my previous friendships. I needed help but thought I was tough enough to handle my pain by making these adult decisions to force my life forward.

On our first night in our apartment, we had a little party with Randy's friends, and after a lifetime of saying no to drugs, that was the night I first tried crystal meth. I'd always heard about it as the skinny drug and secretly wanted to try it, but I was too afraid to admit it. Randy wasn't happy about it. He never liked drugs and was so bothered his friends brought them over that he asked everyone to leave. He told me he cared about me too much to let me get wrapped up in drugs. I saw a different side of Randy that night: angry and erratic. I told myself it was because he cared. Our friendship quickly evolved into a relationship. We spent every moment together, except on the weekends when I worked.

    We weren't the best for each other. We were both spoiled, independent, controlling, and all the other downfalls of only children. We filled the weeks leading up to our Disney trip with laughter and fighting. I was hard to fight with. All the yelling from my mom growing up numbed me to people's aggression, and it frustrated him when he couldn't get a rise out of me. Many nights ended with our bedroom a complete wreck. He would dismantle the bed and pull clothes off hangers. Although he never hit me, he would yell and throw things at me. He would put my five-pound dog on top of the fridge and let her cry just to upset me. I ended up giving her to my parents to avoid that abuse. These episodes would last a few hours before he would feel horrible. Then he would act like the man I always dreamed of. I felt like I could fix him. The good times outweighed the bad. I understand why people stay in abusive relationships. There's always hope of no more fighting.

    Our turning point happened on our Disney trip that April. On our last night in the hotel room, we had one of our biggest fights. He pulled out his gun, which I didn't know he had, and threatened to kill himself in front of me. I remember cowering in a corner, scared out of my mind that he would actually do it, and at the same time, thinking maybe I could kill myself after. When I told him my plan, he snapped back to his remorseful side. He kept saying how sorry he was and that he would never do that again. That I even considered such an act shows how the accumulated trauma was affecting me.

We were both pretty stunned by that evening. On the six-hour drive home the next day, we came up with a new plan. We would move to Illinois, where I had family, and start fresh, away from all the distractions that caused him to be insecure and jealous. His dad gave him a truck that just needed new tires. The only problem was that it was in Flagstaff and would need to be towed to Phoenix for tires. Nothing would stop us. We figured it all out. He would go pick up his truck and get it in running condition, and I would give the car that was in my parents' name back to them and would no longer have that monthly payment. I would continue working weekends and pick up some weekdays so we could leave in June. We hadn't fought since Disney. It was amazing. We celebrated our two-month anniversary and were both so excited about the new life we had planned.

Randy finally found a trailer to borrow to get his truck home from Flagstaff, which was only two hours away. He begged me to go with him, but I always hated that drive, with lots of twists and turns and steep hills, and he wanted to drive at night. So on May 14th, he took one of his friends instead, and I stayed home. I woke up at 4:00 AM and found it odd that he wasn't home yet. I paged him and waited... over an hour later, my phone rang, and I expected it to be him. It was an officer with Randy's pager. He told me he was downstairs and asked if he could come up. As I opened the door, I saw the two officers coming up the stairs. They asked if they could come in. I will never forget the words the officer said to me: Randy had been in an accident. It was fatal, but the passenger was in stable condition. The ground started moving, the room was spinning, and my legs gave out. I fell to the floor and couldn't stop crying. Everything I'd ever hoped for, dreamed of, was gone. I don't know how long I cried or when the officers left. I was in shock. The pain was too much. I honestly wanted to die. Hours later, our friends showed up to be with me. I could not get control of my emotions. My friend gave me a pill that I later learned was Xanax, and I was out.

The next few months were some of my lowest. I got body piercings with friends and I dove into drugs, mainly amphetamines, as well as muscle relaxers, opioids, downers, alcohol, and more. I would be up for days at a time, then crash for days. Sometimes, I would mix all kinds to see what would happen. I wanted to die. There were nights I roamed my apartment complex, knocking on doors, looking for my dog because I forgot I gave her to my parents. I spent hours peeking through my blinds, watching for visitors. I had allowed different dealers to sleep in my bed in exchange for all the meth I wanted. I lost almost 40 pounds in little time. I had never been a thin person, so I loved that. An influx of visitors inundated me, all trying to "save" me. There were my parents, old girl friends, church friends, coworkers. All my guy friends from high school tried to convince me to come back to school, but we would just end up sleeping together before they left.

They probably told each other because they kept coming, one after another. I'm pretty sure I slept with the entire baseball team. I felt almost nothing. It only felt nice to be liked and wanted, as twisted as that sounds.

One dealer who stayed with me got me a job at a strip bar, which was a flop. Then he hooked me up with an escort agency to make easy money. I had no idea what I was getting into. I was naive, but I learned quickly how to stay alive. I ended up in more scary situations than I like to admit, but the money was good. I could pay my bills and keep up with my habit.

In August, my ex-boyfriend of almost three years came to visit me at my apartment. He brought his friend, Nick, with him. He was worried about me. The girl he knew all those years was nowhere to be seen. I know he heard from his friends about my lifestyle. He was hopeful for us to get back together, but I had no interest. That Misty was gone, and anything attached to her was gone as well. Instead, I made friends with Nick. He started coming over without Ryan, and he had no interest in sleeping with me. In fact, he told me he was coming around because he was determined to straighten me out. He said it looked like I needed a friend more than anything, and that's what he wanted to be. He had just started his senior year at my old high school. His older brother was my best friend's boyfriend for a time, and I knew him well. What I knew about Nick was that all the girls liked him, and now he was hanging with me. I definitely liked that feeling. I continued with my escort job and drug use when he wasn't around but led the appearance that I was done with all that. Nick and I became great friends. We would talk all night on the phone, and I would pick him up after school, and we'd hang out most evenings. After about six weeks, we finally slept together and made our relationship public. By this time, I had cut back my addiction. I learned to make myself sleep at night, so I didn't look wired the next day. I didn't let dealers stay with me anymore because I never knew when Nick would show up, and I didn't like the way they made me feel. I had cousins that lived nearby who I knew could help me, so I ended up reaching out to them for my future purchases. They always took good care of me and didn't tell anybody.

Life seemed to normalize. My nine-month tailspin was ending. I was talking to my parents and various old friends again. I pretended to be done with all the drugs and over the loss of Randy, though I was continuously numbing my trauma and grief. Nick and I were growing our relationship the best we knew how. Then the unimaginable happened. A few days before my 19th birthday, I realized my period was late. I took a pregnancy test on my birthday and got the shock of my life—I was pregnant.

HE WAS ALWAYS THERE...

> *"But as for you, you meant evil against me;*
> *but God meant it for good."*
> *- Genesis 50:20 NKJV*

Sometimes, things happen in our lives that break our hearts or steal our joy. In those moments, it is easy to forget that God has a hand in every part of our lives.

I want you to know, in the same way God used the brothers of Joseph in Genesis 50:20, and the evil they did to him, to turn what the enemy meant for evil into good, He will do it for you too! Jesus can heal your mind, your soul, and your spirit from the injustice you endured!

Rape is an injustice. It affects the mind, soul, and spirit. I can look back to both times I was raped and see a shift in the wrong direction. The shame I felt from these two instances kept me from speaking out. This dark secret was the beginning of my life of promiscuity. I spent the next ten years doing all that I could to forget.

But running from the pain in your heart from all your accumulated, unprocessed hurts will cost you. It cost me a year of one bad thing after the other, followed by years of running in the wrong direction. You can only stay non-reactive to trauma for so long before those unresolved things surface and try to destroy you.

Have you ever been raped or sexually abused? Have you blamed yourself or lived in shame for things others did to you, thinking it was your fault? Do you have dark secrets that are eating you up inside? Do you realize you can receive deep healing in your heart and life by bringing these things into the light of God's love, and eventually, perhaps even minister to others who also need healing? Have you ever felt yourself in a downward spiral of destructive behavior, compromising your morals and standards to dull your pain and grief? Jesus stands ready, not only to forgive you, but to wipe the slate clean from your past and give you a brand new start.

# 4
## Motherhood

Pregnant! How could I be pregnant? Why did my birth control pill not work? How was I going to tell Nick? He was still in high school! I just stood there, looking at that test stick, wishing it to change, or hoping I was just seeing double, when there was really only one line. Was I ready for this? Could I stop using drugs just like that? My head was spinning. I sat on the toilet and cried.

That afternoon, my talk with Nick went better than I expected. He was excited. We began talking about marriage and what that would look like. He dropped out of school to get a full-time job. I went back to working nights as a CNA in people's homes rather than the nursing home. Our parents took the news fine as well. We planned a wedding in less than two months and married on February 17th. My parents bought a town home and signed over to us the mortgage of the house I grew up in. Everything came together.

I was thankful to be pregnant, thankful my time with drugs was over. Although pregnancy was physically easy for me, it was tough on my mental state. I hated the weight gain. My chest, belly, and thighs competed to see which one could be the biggest. Other than gaining weight, I didn't struggle with all the normal discomforts that came with pregnancy. To combat my thoughts about being fat, I spent every morning at the gym until the day before I delivered. I felt good, but because of my family health history (which I didn't know wasn't mine), we had to do all the tests available. The test results were always good, but the fears leading up were heavy. Our excitement exponentially grew when we find out we were having a boy.

Married life was good. Most days, I felt like we were playing house. Neither of us grew up in healthy families, but we were trying. I had to adjust to being back in the house where I spent the last bit of my not-so-great childhood. We got an equity loan to repaint the inside and outside and put new flooring throughout the house to change the look. That made a tremendous difference. We used the rest for the baby's nursery and other needs. Old friends from church stopped by to visit often and show support even though I hadn't attended in years.

August finally came, which meant my due date was quickly approaching. At my 39-week exam, my doctor said I was already dilated to two centimeters and fully effaced, which wasn't common for first-time moms. He asked if I was ready to have this baby. I couldn't believe it was finally time. I spent that evening at the gym and did two aerobic classes back-to-back, knowing it would be six weeks before I could workout again. I was so nervous about the delivery. The epidural video haunted me. I couldn't get the size of that needle out of my head, but the thought of the pain without it scared me more.

We arrived at the hospital early the next morning, ready to meet our baby. It turned out my nurse was my long-time friend Allison's mom, Valerie, who was like a second mom to me. This was no coincidence, either. She is the reason I have birthed all my children naturally. The induction started at 7:00 AM. Contractions were slow at first, nothing like I imagined they'd be. After a while, I got in the tub to help with the pain. By 9:00 AM, contractions were every 3-5 minutes, and I was ready for that epidural. Valerie kept telling me to stay in the tub for a few more minutes. At 10:30 AM, I couldn't take it anymore. I wanted an epidural, and no-one was going to talk me out of it this time. Walking to the bed from the tub was almost too much to bear. I couldn't get there quickly enough. Once in bed, Valerie checked me and immediately changed modes. She said there would be no epidural because it was time to push. That unbearable pain was what ten centimeters and a baby crowning felt like. After two pushes, Travis came out. He was a perfect seven-pound, 20-inch bundle of joy. By 4:00 PM, I begged my doctor to discharge us and let us go home. I hated hospitals, and a massive storm was coming. I wanted to go home. I didn't even feel like I just had a baby. Surprisingly, he said yes. Thinking back, I can't believe they let the two of us kids leave the hospital with that little piece of life in our hands. We thought we were so old and knew everything.

Motherhood was great. I was fully devoted to the needs of my baby. He went everywhere with me. I didn't like being away from him. The only sitter he had in his first year was my parents, and that was usually around his nap time or evenings before going to bed. Nick and I were a good team. He changed jobs often, always looking for the next best thing, while I continued working a few nights each week for the home health agency. I started taking Travis to my old church across the street on Sundays. I didn't want him growing up like Nick and I did, with no direction, and it felt good to be surrounded by all the families and friends I grew up with. Nick didn't love the idea, but he didn't stop us from going, either. We reconnected with my old girlfriends, who were all newly married and pregnant with their first babies. It was nice to hang out with other couples in the same season of life. For the first time in a long time, I felt normal. I was no longer the "bad sheep." My life was finally headed in the right direction.

## HE WAS ALWAYS THERE…

Looking back on this year, I can see that God was everywhere, with His protection on my life and that of my new baby. Of course, I remember giving the credit to my driven, independent self. The Lord protected my baby from my drug use in the beginning of my pregnancy. He gave me the perfect nurse, whom He knew I needed to get through labor. The ease of my birth experience set me up for the many pregnancies ahead. Self-reliance can be one of the hardest barriers standing in the way of intimacy with God.

Can you remember an experience in your life when you took all the credit, but can now look back and see that it was God all along? Do you desire deeper intimacy with God? Are you willing to let down your walls of self-protection and self-sufficiency to allow Him in to every area of your life? From my experience, He is trustworthy to handle my heart with care, just as He will do for you.

# 5
## My First Marriage

My one-year wedding anniversary came just two days after I heard the biggest news of my life—news that rocked my world and answered years of tormenting questions. All the people who asked if I was adopted and looked confused when I said no. All the unexplained differences between me and my entire family. I was still in shock. I wondered if my birth mom, Gayle, would call. What would she say? What did she look like? Did I look like her? Technology was different back then; we couldn't just text or e-mail a picture like people can today.

That afternoon, I got the call I had been waiting for. I will never forget when I asked her to describe herself to me. She said she was 5'5" with brown hair and had always been told she had the biggest brown eyes. This excited me because those things were true for me as well. I sat there imagining what she looked like. She told me she was very young when she had me and wasn't ready to be a mom. Her relationship with my birth father ended when I was born, but he was still alive. She still lived in Iowa, and I had two half-siblings who lived with their dad six hours from me in California. Brittany was almost 11 and Caanan was 12. I was so ready to meet them. Not only was this day my anniversary, but I soon learned it was also Gayle's birthday... what a wink from God!

Caanan and Brittany's dad said they could spend their spring break with me if we came and picked them up. I was surprised he would let them go with a stranger but wasn't going to question it. They were just as excited to meet me as I was them. Gayle had told them about me a few years earlier, so they had been waiting longer than me. I had always wanted siblings, and this filled empty holes within me.

The next month, Travis and I flew to Illinois to meet my birth parents. By this time, I had seen pictures of them, but I was really excited to spend time with my birth mom. We had so many similarities that it scared me. We had the same tendencies, thought processes, and struggles. Many times, our conversations would send me into a tailspin of thoughts, wondering why I should even try to be good. After all these years, she was still struggling, and I was just like her, so why waste my energy if I was going to end up in the same place? The enemy had finally found a way back into my thoughts. I met my birth dad and his family, and I learned where I got my olive skin and all my curves.

When I returned home, life subsided. I hired a personal trainer at the gym to help me shed the rest of my pregnancy weight. Nick delivered pizzas while still trying every get-rich-quick scheme that came our way. We didn't tend our marriage well. Neither one of us grew up with a good example to follow. I would express my concern, he would say we were better than most couples, and we would continue on. I always dreamed of a marriage like in the movies.

I longed to be kissed passionately, like Tom Cruise kissed Kelly McGillis in *Top Gun* or Richard Gere kissed Julia Roberts in *Pretty Woman*. Nick told me those only existed in the movies. I started believing he was right.

We had no wiggle room in our finances. When I told my trainer I had to take a break because I couldn't afford training, he told me about his client looking to hire someone to help in the afternoons. I was interested. Travis napped in the afternoons, so the timing could be perfect.

The interview did not go as I expected. My trainer misled me. His client wasn't looking for someone to work part-time in the afternoons, but rather someone to pose in photographs and perform sexual favors. I was disgusted. This married man wanted to pay me to let him take whatever pictures he wanted and have his way with me. Were all men like this? Why couldn't his wife fill this role at no cost? I still knew so little about the world. He could tell I had no idea what I walked in to. He asked me to hear him out and think about it. There was no way I would think about anything... or so I thought.

I couldn't get the numbers out of my head. I could make about $2,000 a month with just two visits a week. That was equal to mine and Nick's combined income. To double our income that easily was hard to pass up. I convinced myself that I had to do it for just a while to get us ahead. It was one of the hardest things I stepped into. As weeks passed, it got easier. I learned how to put those acts in a compartment buried so deep, I couldn't even find it. I wished Nick would notice something, anything, but he just wasn't that perceptive. He loved that money was no longer a stress and never asked me about the job.

I took the enemy's bait here! I should've walked out of that office as soon as I realized what the job was. But I kept the door propped open. That's where the enemy got me—that little decision brought great danger.

Our marriage slowly faded during the months that passed. Nick refused to see any problems. His response was always that we were better than most. In hindsight, I can see we had different perspectives on what a good marriage looked like. The thought of divorce haunted me. Failure was knocking on my door again.

That following summer, Nick and I needed some time apart. Travis and I took a trip to Illinois to visit family. There were moments I was so sad about my failing marriage that I imagined leaving Travis with a family member and driving to the woods to take my life. My emotions were convinced that was the best solution, but when I thought about who would take care of Travis, I couldn't do it.

My mom, Gayle, lived with her boyfriend and his son. This time, my visit took a different turn. I was no longer breastfeeding, so I had more freedom. We went out one night and both ended up sick in the bathroom, too drunk to drive home. It was my first time drinking since all those years ago, so it didn't take much. Gayle asked me if I'd ever tried cocaine. She said it would sober us up so we could get home. I would do anything to make the spinning stop. After one line up the nose, the spinning stopped, and in minutes, I felt normal. It was invigorating. All my memories of doing meth came swirling back.

I felt disappointed with myself the next morning because I liked it. I had fun with Gayle, and we connected differently. I justified my actions by saying I was on vacation, and it was okay to have a little fun. I knew I would be fine when I got back home, although I couldn't stop thinking about the few extra pounds I could lose with little effort.

After being gone almost six weeks, it was time for us to return home. I hated I didn't miss or even think about Nick much during that time. When we arrived home, we said hi and gave each other an awkward hug. After a few days, I gave in to my urges and called one of my cousins to see what they had on hand. They only had crack-cocaine. I hadn't heard of that before. They told me it was a mix of meth and cocaine, and the only difference was how you smoked it. I made the mistake of trying it. I was instantly hooked. I picked up an extra visit at the office to pay for my new habit. By this time, Nick and I were more like roommates. We never fought; we just rarely talked about anything important. Neither one of us was happy, but we had no idea what to do about it, so time just kept moving forward.

Months later, we got our next big shock. I was pregnant again. I was not excited this time. The thought of bringing another baby into whatever we had going on scared me. I had been a functioning addict for about four months now. I had no idea how far along I was because I couldn't remember the last time I had a period. I was honest with my doctor about my drug use so they could hold me accountable. Travis spent quite a few days at my parents' house during that time while I slept my way through detoxing. My doctor prescribed me some antidepressants to help me get through.

Although this pregnancy felt like my shortest one, it was my most difficult, emotionally and physically. I was almost 20 weeks when I found out, and then at 28 weeks, due to my drug use early on, I was told I had placenta previa, and my worst nightmare was going to come true: I had to have a c-section. I started spotting around 30 weeks. I was put on bed rest but didn't take it too seriously, fully unaware of the severity. The rule was every time I had enough blood to fill a pad, I had to head to the hospital, which was 25 minutes away. I was driving to the hospital 3-4 times a week. It was exhausting. So at 33 weeks, after multiple steroid shots, we did an amnio to check lung development. The alternative was to admit me, and I was fighting hard against that one. Hours later, while waiting for the results, I felt warm liquid gushing out of me. I could see by the look on Nick's face and the face of the nurses that something was terribly wrong. Everything else was a blur. I woke up to the news that Bryana was a healthy baby girl at 5 pounds, 2 ounces. Had I not been in the hospital already, my doctor said we wouldn't have survived.

Nick and I decided we needed a fresh start. We needed to make some changes if this family was going to make it. We sold the house and moved into an apartment while we waited for our new house to be built. We dove into the Mormon church, because that is all I really knew, and started taking temple prep classes in hopes to better our marriage. I took a break from my "office" job. We tried to do all the right things. He still wouldn't pay for counseling, but we were confident that what we were doing was making a difference. We finished the temple classes and scheduled the day to be sealed in the local Mormon temple. We moved into our new house around the same time. I think we both convinced ourselves that this would change everything. When it didn't, the disappointment hit us hard.

All this time, attending church did nothing for my soul. I remember just going through the motions, hoping things would change. No one ever talked about a relationship with Jesus, or if they did, I didn't hear them. Mormons believe they are saved by works, so as long as we do the right things, we're good. I have since learned we are saved by grace, and grace alone! I love Ephesians 2:8 in the Passion Translation: "For by grace you have been saved by faith. Nothing you did could ever earn this salvation, for it was the love gift from God that brought us to Christ!"

The new house put us in over our heads financially. I had to go back to my "office" job to make ends meet. After Bryana turned one, I tried these new fat burners the guy at the supplement store told me were magic pills. He was so right. I dropped weight instantly. I should've stopped after my first bottle, but loved watching the scale drop daily. I justified this because it was legal. I wasn't hiding them, except for maybe how many I was taking. Unfortunately, these pills put me in the ICU for over a week. I was told it was pretty scary in the beginning, and I almost didn't pull though. Oh, the shame I felt that time. It was heavy.

A nice mom of seven, from church, took care of our kids while I was in the hospital. After I was discharged, I had a severe allergic reaction to all the fluids. I blew up like a balloon, gained 35 pounds, and broke out all over my body. I spent my first few days at their house so she could help. She was so sweet. The energy from all the kids running around felt good. I will never forget my conversation with her that day. She had been married for 13 years. I asked her if she loved her marriage, if it was everything she'd hoped it to be. She told me love is a decision, and whether she was over-the-top happy or not, it didn't matter. This was the life she had, and she would choose to be happy. That was tough for me to swallow. The thought of another 10 years in my current marriage made my stomach turn.

We continued attending church on Sundays, pretending like we were great, but we were drifting further and further apart. I couldn't remember the last time we were intimate. We just stopped initiating. We didn't have the tools needed to fix all the broken areas. We had let too many walls go up and too many words be said to know where to start. Then there was pride. People thought we had a good marriage. Everyone thought we were this cute little family. I started selling Pampered Chef, which had me out of the house multiple evenings a week, and then on the extra evenings, I took ballroom dancing lessons. For the next several months, we lived as roommates and rarely spent time as a family.

Things finally came to a head in February 2002, days before our sixth anniversary. We had a pretty big fight, and Nick left his ring with a note on the counter, saying he was done. While I knew he was only trying to get my attention, I took this opportunity to be done as well. I placed my ring next to his, packed a few things, grabbed my kids and headed to my aunt's house. I felt relieved, and then I felt guilty about it. My marriage was over, and all I felt was relief.

## HE WAS ALWAYS THERE...

One of my favorite things about God is how He blesses us even when we don't acknowledge Him. My pregnancy with Bryana has Him written all over it. I was 20 weeks along when I found out. It pains me to admit that I was doing drugs all that time and had no idea a baby was growing inside of me. In God's mercy, she was born healthy. Had I not spotted enough that morning to head to the hospital, neither one of us would've survived. My diet pill episode that put me in the ICU for over a week was another unexplained pull-through. No matter how many church things we attended, I still always chose the wide path... the wrong one. Religion didn't have the power to change my heart but fooled me into thinking it had. Once I no longer behaved like I was supposed to, God and others rejected me. Yet, God saved my life repeatedly, like a patient, loving Father, waiting for me to turn to Him.

Was there a time in your life when you weren't walking with God, but as you look back now, you can see His hand was keeping you safe and guiding you until a time you could make things truly right with Him? Have you done that? Have you exchanged religious activities for a true relationship with Him? His love covers every mistake you have ever made and wipes it clean. He truly has been there all along.

# 6
## Clearing the Slate

By age 25, I was divorced with two kids, trying to figure things out on my own. I was damaged. After my church told me I could not come back unless I reconciled my marriage, while they embraced Nick with love and acceptance, I had no faith left. For some, doing whatever it takes to fix their marriage is the right choice, but I knew we were never the best for each other. We were young and dumb and tried to fix our mistake by getting married, without knowing we were making another mistake. Now I felt I didn't need a man in my life, anyway. Relationships took work, and I was tired. My "office" job covered all my expenses with extra left over, so I took a break from Pampered Chef shows and focused on being the best mom I could be.

Divorce brought unexpected changes. Some friends chose Nick's side and some mine, but never both. I didn't understand why there had to be sides. His entire family disowned me, which was tough to swallow. Because we kept the condition of our marriage a secret, our separation shocked everyone, including our kids. I didn't do the best job of protecting their hearts through that time. I was still such a kid myself but thought I knew everything.

I am still seeing the consequences of my early parenting years with my first two kids.

A few weeks after Nick and I separated, a friend told me about a new online dating platform called Matchmaker. She was 10 years older than me and struggled with technology. She had been divorced for years and was ready to meet someone. She wanted me to help her make a profile, and make one for myself. I told her more than once I was enjoying life without a man. She thought I could only answer all her questions if I had my own profile, and she was right. I didn't feel ready, but I caved. I made the profiles but didn't put a picture on mine for a few days. After she complained, I uploaded my picture. The platform matched people based on their answers to questions. My strongest match was a good-looking guy named Matt. He and I started messaging through the site on Easter weekend in 2002. It was my first holiday without my kids, and I was lonely. I figured it was harmless. (Little did I know this would be the man I would have seven more babies with.)

My sister, Brittany, was also messaging me about her visit the following week. She asked if we could go on a double date. My first thought was a quick "no," until I remembered the guy from Matchmaker. I messaged him and told him I'd go on a double date with him if he found a friend around 18 for my sister. I hadn't talked to any other guys from that site, let alone given out my address, so this was a stretch. He responded within the hour that he found a friend, and they would pick us up on Tuesday, which was only two days away. What was I getting myself into this time? I told myself it was all to give Brittany a good time.

I picked her up from the airport Tuesday morning. We spent the day getting ready for our date that night. As we waited outside, I was so nervous. She was the opposite... giddy and excited. I had never been on a blind date. What if they were disappointed when they arrived? What if we were? What if they were creeps? There was no turning back. Then it happened. A big, white, lifted F150 stopped in front of my building, and two guys got out and walked toward us. My heart skipped a beat, and I was taken aback. That had never happened to me before. I just assumed it was from the excitement of the situation. Brittany and Preston broke the awkward silence with their bubbly giggles. Matt and I said hi and headed to his truck.

We planned the evening at a complex called Desert Ridge filled with restaurants, shops, and a Dave & Busters. Throughout dinner, Brittany kept kicking me under the table or nudging me to get closer to Matt. Meanwhile, she and Preston made out the entire time. It gave us something to laugh about throughout dinner. We then headed to the arcade to play games. I loved video games, and I was good, so I pretty much beat Matt at every game. The other two stayed outside, making out most of the evening until it was time to go home. They definitely kept us laughing. Matt grabbed my hand a few times, and I hated that I liked it. When we got back to my place, I invited them to come in for a drink. Matt and I headed out to the patio while Brittany and Preston stayed inside. We stood out there talking on the patio for hours. The things I was feeling inside were so foreign. My stomach was in knots. The air between us was thick. At 4:00 AM, he finally kissed me, and I thought I was going to pass out. My insides were on fire. Never in my life had I felt anything like I did in that moment. We spent the night together, and it was unlike anything I had ever experienced. Until that night, I had had sex with others, but this was not just sex—it was intimacy.

The next morning, they headed home, and I was still dazed and confused. I was so ashamed for sleeping with a guy the first night we met. I told Brittany I could not see him again. It was too dangerous. He played with my heartstrings too much, and I didn't want to get in over my head. She thought I was nuts and told me to have a little fun. My life was still complicated. I had too many secrets, and having people close to me made it more difficult to keep those secrets, but she didn't know that because I kept them from her as well.

A couple days later, Matt called and asked if he could take me and my kids to Peter Piper Pizza for dinner. I gave a quick "no," and then told him it's best we not involve my kids. He said it was too late; he was already outside. He drove 50 miles to take us to dinner. Was I really going to tell him no? I didn't think I would see him again. Boy, was I wrong. Dinner was fun. My kids had a blast. He taught them how to spit balls out of a straw. He made them laugh a lot. I remember sitting there scared out of my mind about the things I was feeling inside. I wanted to run away.

That night, after I got the kids to bed, we sat on the couch and talked for hours. First, he apologized for sleeping with me on our first night together. He said he had never done that before. He went on to say he felt things for me he's never felt for anyone and believed the feelings were mutual. I was dumbfounded. I finally told him I wasn't divorced yet, thinking that would scare him away. Instead, he spent the night again, and that night was even better than the first. There was an energy between us so strong, neither of us could deny it. He consumed my thoughts. I kept thinking we would have a little more fun and then go in our separate directions. The days turned into weeks, and May came. Since he slept over every night anyway, he decided to move in to my little apartment. After a couple weeks, we looked for a house to rent, and by June, we had moved.

Yes, people thought we were nuts. The few friends I had in my life were convinced I was not in my right mind. In fact, one of my friend's husbands told Matt to run far from me because I had way too much baggage. Nick was not happy about another man living with his kids, understandably. Matt's parents strongly expressed their disapproval as well. Heck, I wouldn't have approved either. I had so many issues I hadn't dealt with yet. There were so many challenges that could resurface.

Weekends without the kids turned into mini vacations. I still hadn't told him about my struggles with addiction or the ICU incident that happened just over a year ago; so he didn't think twice about asking me if I wanted to try some X while in Vegas. I wanted to try it. My body had a slight reaction that evening, but everything turned out okay. I reassured him it was no big deal. A couple of weeks later, we went to Mexico and did more X. I didn't feel bad about using drugs with him because we only did it on vacation and not in our "real" life.

My "office" job was a lot harder for me to go to for many reasons. I had never felt guilty before until Matt. I hated that feeling. He asked more questions about it, for which I had to make up answers. He would notice how long I was gone, so I would have to stay away longer and hide some of the money. I wanted it to be over more than ever. I hated lying to him.

On August 26th, we had Travis's school orientation. It got over a little later than usual and instead of heading home, Matt drove toward the mall. I got a little irritated because it was a school night, and I wanted Travis to get to bed at a decent time. I was bothered he couldn't be more specific about what he needed from the mall that night. He ran in while I pouted in the car with the kids. A few minutes later, he returned and came to me on my side of the truck. He opened a ring box in front of me and said these words: "Misty, I know things have been crazy fast for us, and I may not be able to give you the life you've always wanted, but no one will love you more than I do. Will you marry me?" I sat there staring at him. I wanted to punch him for letting me act like such a brat. Thinking of my first marriage, I learned everything about what not to do. I did so many things wrong and let things go too far. I was confident I could make this one work. Excitedly, I said yes. We still had to wait for my divorce to finalize before we could set a date, but the excitement was real. His parents asked if we would wait until January so they could come. So we set a tentative date of January 19th, believing that date would be safe. We got notice in early October that my divorce was final.

The following month, Matt took a job in Tucson, 100 miles away from us. It was a two-month job that ended up taking four, but it paid well. In the beginning, he would drive to and from work each day just because we couldn't stand to be apart. Eventually, it made more sense to only come home for the weekends. All this down time during the week was new to me. After one of our fun weekends, we had some cocaine left over. I thought about wanting to be thin for our wedding, so I ended up doing it. Soon I was back to doing it regularly while the kids were at school.

Hiding my addiction from Matt was more difficult than I expected. He noticed more things, like my pupils and various quirks. I didn't even try to do it on the weekends when he was home unless he was the one to get it because he was way too perceptive. In December, my worst nightmare happened. Somehow, he found my stash and asked me about it. I denied knowing anything about it and conjured up anger towards him for thinking I would do such a thing. This infuriated him. I had never seen him so mad. The hurt look on his face is unforgettable. He stormed off, and I really didn't know if he was coming back. I decided he deserved someone better. This addiction would always come back to haunt me. I would never be free of it, and it wasn't fair for me to drag anyone down with me.

I sat in the garage and cried. What was wrong with me? Instead of apologizing and telling him the truth, I turned it on him. When he pulled in the driveway and came in the garage, I told him it was over before he could say anything. I would probably always choose drugs first, I announced; therefore, he was better off without me. He sat at my feet and put his head in my lap and cried. I had never seen him cry. It was too much. He blamed himself for bringing drugs back into my life and for taking the long-distance job. He told me he was in it for the long haul. At that moment, I wished more than ever that I could say I would never do drugs again.

With wedding plans in full swing, the date was approaching fast. On New Year's Day, we got another surprise. We were pregnant. It turns out drugs negate the effects of birth control. This was my third time getting pregnant on the pill. I was frustrated because I wanted to do things in the right order this time, meaning first get married, then get pregnant. The upside was I had to stop using drugs. We kept that secret to ourselves until after the wedding to avoid all the assumptions.

Our wedding was absolutely perfect. We invited 40 of our closest friends and family and rented out a little wedding chapel. My parents were still paying off my first wedding, so we were on our own funding this one, but it was worth it. For our honeymoon, we spent a couple nights at a resort nearby. We spent hours talking about our future and all that we hoped for.

Since we were already living like a married couple, the only thing that changed after our wedding was my last name. The Tucson job was over, so there was no more traveling. My pregnancy was physically easy. What I battled were the mental struggles. Matt was filled with excitement. He loved rubbing my belly and talking to it every chance he got. Finding out she was a girl made things even more exciting and real for him.

In April, his parents reached out and asked if we'd be open to moving to Florida. They planted roots in a place called Fort Walton Beach. They invited us to live with them until we found a place. When I looked it up, all it said was they had the most beautiful white sandy beaches in America. I never cared for the beach, but my only experience was the Pacific Coast, which is always freezing with rough brown sand. I had been in the Phoenix valley for over 20 years. The thought of leaving both frightened and excited me. The more we thought about it, the more we fell in love with the idea. If I could escape all my triggers, then maybe I wouldn't fall back into my addiction after this pregnancy. I know we both had that unspoken fear. This meant no more "office" job! I offered to waive child support if Nick would let me take the kids to Florida. I knew he would say yes. Sadly, I also knew it would be one of his biggest regrets, but I didn't care because I wanted our family to have a chance at something bigger. I was pretty sure we needed to move away for that to happen. I was sad to be moving so far from my siblings, but I knew this was the right decision.

On July 3rd 2003, at 30 weeks pregnant, we loaded up and said goodbye to the only place I knew as home. After 26 hours of driving, we arrived on July 4th at the Cayo Grand in Fort Walton Beach, Florida, expectant for the next season. Little did we know, we had just landed in the Bible Belt, right where the Lord wanted us.

## HE WAS ALWAYS THERE...

I have concluded my first marriage was the sum of all my poor decisions and unprocessed trauma. The only good that came from it were Travis and Bryana, and lots of lessons learned. I know with everything in me that Matt is the one the Lord always intended for me. I know some don't believe in love at first sight or soul mates, and I don't think I did either, until I met Matt. When we met, one of our first questions was how we felt about God, and we both had the same answer: yes, He is real, but we are fine without Him. I chuckle when I see His workings all around us. We did not even follow God yet, but He helped us find one another. God knew I needed to get out of Arizona and, of all places, he brought us to the panhandle of Florida, the Bible Belt. I love looking back and finding all the places God was with me.

Are there seasons in your life when you feel you reaped from the bad decisions or negative choices you made? Can you now see that these times were detours from what God actually had for you? A beautiful thing about God is that He has a way of making our crooked places straight and redeeming even ungodly choices. He made all things new for me. He can do the same for you.

# 7
## New Beginnings

I couldn't get out of the car fast enough. My legs looked like those of an elephant, no ankles to be seen. My back hadn't stopped aching for the last seven hours of the trip. People were everywhere. Traffic was pretty insane, but then I realized it was the Fourth of July. We heard the sounds of fireworks all around. We made it!

We had a few surprises when we arrived. His parents lived in a two-story condo on the third floor with no elevators. Since they were building a house, all their furniture was still in storage, so everyone slept on air mattresses. I was 30 weeks pregnant and already struggled to get out of normal beds to pee at night, let alone an air mattress. The only way up was to roll myself over onto all fours and then stand up. Another challenging detail was all four of us would be in the same room. Yikes! What had we gotten ourselves into? We were thankful they made a place for us, but it would not be easy. Matt wanted to head on to Orlando to see what we could find there. I refused to get back in that car to go anywhere!

I remember the first day we drove down Highway 98 from Fort Walton Beach. There was so much traffic. We were unaware this was a tourist town. We pulled into Chick-fil-A to feed the kids. Sitting there surrounded by people with strong southern accents made me wonder what we got ourselves into. I didn't know most of them weren't locals; I just knew we stood out like sore thumbs. We went on to explore more. Where were all the stores, the malls, the theaters, the restaurants, the big city things? There was one Walmart, one Target, one Chick-fil-A, all on one main road, and none of my favorite little conveniences I was used to. I freaked out. This was a culture shock!

We spent the next week trying to find Matt a job. We drove up and down Highway 98, calling numbers off the signs from all the large commercial construction jobs, only to learn none of those companies were local. It frustrated me that we were wasting our time. What if there were no jobs that paid what we needed? I grew tired of driving around aimlessly with him, so while he was out one day, I grabbed a big phone book and opened to the contractors section. I started at A and went down the list, asking if they were looking to hire a superintendent or project manager. The fact that I was a girl always got their attention, until I told them I was calling for my husband. I got through all the A's with no luck. I was a little discouraged. What was I thinking? Cold calling! And then there was light. I got to Breaux Construction and said the same thing I'd been saying. By now, it was automatic. I ask, they say no, and I hang up and call the next number. But when I called Breaux Construction, I asked my question, and the lady on the other end actually said yes. I almost didn't know what to do next. I told her a little about Matt and his work experience and then set an interview for the next morning. The downside was it was in Grayton Beach, which was over an hour from where we were living, but it was our only option. It had been almost two weeks, and he needed to work.

The interview was a success, and he started work immediately. Now that we knew what we had to work with to look for a home. In our short couple of weeks there, we knew we didn't want to live in Fort Walton Beach or Destin. Niceville and Bluewater Bay, which were about 20 minutes away, were more family-friendly. We found a 1000—square—foot town home in our price range in Bluewater Bay, which was my top choice. We got the kids enrolled in school and preschool, moved in, and two weeks later, on August 31st, we welcomed Dilan into the world.

We had many adjustments during those first few months. Matt's weekdays at work were long because of his hour-plus commute, so it was just me taking care of our three kids. Finances were tighter than expected. We picked up a weekly paper route for an extra $75 a week for food. Travis and Bryana were in school all day, so I spent most days watching Dawson's Creek with my new baby. On our first time going to the park, I met another mom who had two girls the same age as mine. It turned out we lived a couple of minutes apart. That friend was just what I needed. We started meeting up a few times a week, hanging out as families and then as couples.

As Dilan got older, I noticed there were no indoor play places for toddlers like we had in Phoenix. The closest Gymboree (a reputable indoor play place) was in Pensacola, over an hour away. After lots of thinking, we opened one of our own in Destin. Matt's boss offered to loan us $50,000 to get it started. The Gymboree name was too expensive, so we came up with our own, Under D' Sea. The plan was I would run it while Matt kept his day job. When people asked how I was going to run the business and take care of my three kids, my response was always the same: "Easy! I will hire employees." Boy, I had a lot to learn.

We found our location but had a long road ahead of us before we could open. During that time, Matt's younger brother from Dallas, Eric, was having some struggles at home and needed a place to stay for a while, so he came to live with us. This was one of our many bad decisions. Had we known he struggled with drug use, we might've chosen differently. We allowed him to share a room with Travis, who was eight years old. Matt and I were young parents who didn't know what we were doing. That we put a troubled 18-year-old with our eight-year-old for any length of time baffles me today.

I hadn't really thought about drugs since finding out I was pregnant. That I was still breastfeeding was probably the reason, but I gave myself more credit than that. We made time to exercise to help quiet the voices in my head. It also helped that I didn't have someone I could easily call to get some. I truly believed that part of my life was over… until the day Eric was talking to me about getting high that week. While he slept, I grabbed his phone and got the number of his drug contact. I told myself I would not call, but going from all the freedom to working seven days a week, learning to run a business, leaving no time for exercise, mounted pressure on me. I eventually called the number. For the first time since moving to Florida, I had a bag of meth in my hands. Changing zip codes did not change my heart.

Months passed, and our building was coming along. We spent our weekends there painting the walls and putting together equipment. I started interviewing prospects. During the project, I successfully hid my drug use. I didn't smoke it to avoid having extra things to hide. My weight loss was gradual enough to seem like it was just from all the new stressors. I started shoplifting again just to add to my mound of secrets. It gave me a high that could only come from stealing something.

We signed our papers on December 14, 2004 (my birthday), and officially opened in January. I had no idea what I was doing. I had never run a business before, or hired employees, or had to deal with customers. Having Destin moms as customers tried my patience. Employees did so even more. I quickly learned that while the boss is away, employees will play, so I always had to be present. Running a business was strenuous.

The kids quickly grew tired of being there seven days a week. I missed volunteering at school and going on field trips. I never wanted to be a working mom. I was thankful we were closed on Sundays, but we still had to be there to clean and get ready for the week. During our first month open, our bridge tolls topped $400. We knew the wise thing to do would be to move to Destin. I was sad to make the kids change schools again, but we didn't really have another choice.

I had done a good job of hiding my addiction. I justified it because I felt like I was in complete control. I did a little each morning, and it got me through the day. As long as I didn't do it in the afternoon, my pupils would be normal, and I would be able to sleep that night. Whenever I felt guilty, I reassure myself that it was okay because I wasn't a full-blown druggy like before.

As summer approached, life seemed to normalize. Matt was studying to get his Contractor License. Our business was prospering. We were breaking even each month (even with me skimming cash off the top), which is huge for our first year. The summer flew and school was back in full swing. We enrolled Dilan in a new preschool called Gateway that had a class for two-year-olds a couple of days a week, which helped me tremendously. Travis' birthday request that year was to sell the business so mom could be home again, and so we could find a church to attend on Sundays. We were not expecting those requests. The first one broke my heart.

After lots of thinking, we decided to sell the business. Everyone, including the broker, told us it would be next to impossible to sell so soon. But I started imagining life before Under D' Sea and had convinced myself that I would stop using drugs once I had time to work out and eat right again. As for the request to attend church, we would wait to figure that one out.

Matt found my stash, but I lied and said it must be Eric's because there was no way I would use drugs again. I played the part well, and he believed me. The primary rule for Eric to stay with us was no drugs, which he had been doing from the start, but Matt didn't know. He was forced to move out. I felt a tinge of guilt for lying, but I knew he'd be fine, and honestly, I was tired of him living with us.

Weeks passed with no offers on the business. To combat the stress, I made shoplifting a daily activity. I had never been caught until one day in November 2005. As I left the store, authorities met me and took me into their security room, which was unseen until the door opened. I sat in that room with security as they looked at my license and asked what my real name was. I wanted to be anyone but the real me at that moment. For the first time, the real me was seen by others. There was no way out. All I could think of was my kids in school and Dilan napping with my employee while everyone wonders what happened to me. They accused me of having a fake license, along with other things. That's when Officer Lynch entered the tiny room—sadly, he knew me as a mom and a business owner. Now, my truth was being shown to someone I knew. The security guard told him their accusations, and he immediately confirmed my identity and their falsities. Fortunately, the things I stole totaled less than $50 in value, so the officer took it from there.

As we walked to his car, all I wanted to do was run away and never come back. I didn't think I could face this. I stood there waiting for the handcuffs. He asked me why I did it, and I didn't have an answer. What was I supposed to say, "Everyday I steal something to make myself feel better"? My head was spinning, and I thought I was going to have a panic attack. The officer said, "Today, I am going to show you some grace because I believe that this will be the last time you ever shoplift." I just stared at him, hoping this meant I was free to go. He went on to say, "I am going to arrest you on paper, and you will be required to be in court next month." My court date would be on my birthday. I couldn't get to my car fast enough. I burst into tears. I knew he was right about one thing. I was never going to shoplift again. But I couldn't get the word "grace" out of my head.

That same week, Matt found my stash again. He said he saw a vision of the hiding place. I denied it and claimed it had to be left behind by Eric, which was so ridiculous. The lies were weighing on us. The betrayal was tearing us apart. We fought more often. When he found my stash the third time because of another vision, I thought he was going to lose it when he punched a hole in the wall. I will never forget when I asked him if he could just be okay with me doing a little each day. I told him I had it under control, and if he could just look the other way, things would be so much easier. He looked at me like I had three heads and then told me, "No way!"

December had come, and I was tired. I didn't know how much longer I could keep going. Things were falling apart. But our buyers finally came, seemingly from nowhere. On their first visit to Under D' Sea, we chatted while their kids played, and I mentioned we had been trying to sell for a while. Their ears perked up. They asked a few questions, and to my surprise, they came back a few days later wanting to buy it. So on December 14, exactly one year later, we sold the business with plans to turn it over in January. That same day, I stood in court and pleaded guilty to shoplifting as well. Life was definitely moving in a new direction.

## HE WAS ALWAYS THERE...

I can see God throughout every detail of this chapter, beginning with the job I found Matt by cold-calling. That boss was instrumental in many of our seasons. He taught Matt so much about building, and then decided to gift his original loan of $50,000 to start a business that we sold in a year, helped Matt get his own Florida license, and then gave us his blessing in starting our own company. People like that are rare. We had the favor of God and were completely unaware of it. When I got caught shoplifting, it was no coincidence that my court date was on my birthday, as well as the date we sold our business. It was enough to get my attention. The Lord was pinging Matt's conscience with the desire to be better before I was ready. He gave Matt visions and dreams of where I hid my drugs, even though Matt didn't know Him. The buyers for our business may have appeared to come out of nowhere, but I believe the Lord was waiting for the perfect moment. Our hearts were softening a bit, and God moved in fast.

Can you recognize times in your life when God's hand moved in your favor? Think about it. A loving Father would go out of His way to do things for His kids, whether or not they gave Him credit for it. Make a list of times you know God blessed you, regardless of if you knew Him.

# 8
## The Year I Couldn't Hide

On New Year's Day, 2006, Matt and I made a pact at the beach to start fresh. No more lies, no more drugs... at least that he knew of. We planned to try a church out in February. We both needed some time to adjust to the idea. Our kids were definitely more excited about it than we were. We both believed in God but didn't feel a need for a "higher power" in our lives. I was still using drugs, carefully. I feared getting caught again since we made that pact.

On the first Sunday in February, we went to Destiny Worship Center because that's where Dilan's school was, and we already knew so many people who went there. I had never been in a worship service like theirs. I was used to singing hymns in a Mormon church. This was completely different. All the feelings were too much. I ran to the bathroom and couldn't stop crying. I stayed in there until the music stopped. The message series that month was called Super Bowl Marriage. It rocked our world. We were so captivated by that series that we kept coming back. But in March, I found myself pretending to be sick, mad, or have nothing to wear, so Matt would take the family to church while I stayed home to do my thing. Three months had passed without Matt catching me using drugs. I had gotten good at hiding, but the guilt was tearing me apart, and it was even worse at church. I later realized that this was the Lord drawing me in.

During the last week of March, we took a family vacation with some other families to Disney for five days. I was nervous to not be able to do drugs for that long but excited to see if I could do it. By the third day, Matt noticed my sleeping was strange. I think that is when he first doubted I was keeping my pact. I couldn't stop, so I knew I had to be extra careful.

In April, a group of ladies at a birthday dinner invited me to go to the beach the next day. It seemed casual since it was with a group. I still didn't have any close, intimate relationships for fear of exposing all my secrets. The only problem was, by God's design, I was the only one who showed up with the birthday girl that day at the beach.

As Karen and I sat there talking, we were all over the place. I loved that she had her Bible right there with her. I always admired good Christian women. Their faith impressed me. I felt like I gave God a chance all the years I went to the Mormon church. It just didn't work for me. I had done way too many things in my life, and I didn't need anyone to rely on… all lies I believed. We talked about how she became a Christian and her choices in life before Jesus. We talked about drugs and alcohol and parties. She asked when I had last done drugs. When I tried to answer, nothing came out. Something was wrong. I couldn't speak. After a very long pause, I finally uttered, "I did the last of what I had this morning." I just sat there frozen, thinking about what just came out of my mouth.

Why did I say that? The look on her face! She asked me what I did. I thought, I can save myself right here and say diet pills or even marijuana... anything but the truth. I could not tell her the truth or my life would be ruined. But my mouth started moving without my control, and the words that came out were, "I've been doing crystal meth for the last 18 months." I said that, while I have tried to stop, I have been unsuccessful, but it's okay because I have it under control. The look on her face was complete shock. I was still stunned myself. I had never in my life admitted my addiction out loud to anyone. I wanted to get up and leave. The silence was too much.

She asked me if I believed in Jesus. The truth was I believed God created us, and Jesus was God's son, and good people go to heaven. But I had my fill of religion. I tried living right, and it didn't change me, and I didn't need that in my life like some people. She told me Jesus could heal me from my addiction. At that point, she lost me. It was time for me to go pick up my kids. She grabbed my hands and started praying for me, asking Jesus to take the desire from me. I couldn't get away fast enough. On my way to the school, I was hoping it was all a bad dream because if it wasn't, I was in a heap of trouble.

Karen called that evening, and I was so scared she was going to tell Matt about our conversation. Instead, she invited me to her house the next morning. I would do anything to keep her quiet. Our other friend, Mary, took Dilan to her house to play so we could talk. My fear of Mary being upset about the news ended with her hugging me and telling me she loved me. This was all very strange. I was expecting a much different response. Karen handed me the phone and said the first thing we're going to do is call the pastor's wife. I was thinking, "no way." I had spent the last year smiling and shaking her hand at various school events and on Sundays. How was I supposed to tell her I've been doing drugs the whole time? I was terrified. My strongest hope was that she wouldn't answer… but she did. I stuttered over my words and was finally able to tell her who I was. There was no way to avoid it, so I just said, "I've been struggling with a meth addiction for the last 18 months, and I need help." Her response was nothing like I imagined. No shaming or judging. Instead, she asked me if I owned a Bible and a good devotional. I had neither. She said that was my first assignment. She told me I needed to pick some verses from the Bible that encouraged me and write them on note cards. I needed to remove anything secular from my life: TV shows, movies, music. Lastly, I needed to tell my husband. It felt good to tell someone. It felt even better seeing their responses. I left her house that day filled with different emotions. I had a glimmer of hope peeking its way out that this might actually work, but my familiar thoughts said otherwise.

We spent the next day doing much of the same as the previous—lots of praying, reading the Bible, and finding verses and songs that could encourage and strengthen me. I wrote them down on note cards to look at throughout the day. I was getting nervous as the days passed. Usually by the third or fourth day without drugs, getting out of bed was next to impossible. We decided that Thursday night Karen would watch my kids so I could tell Matt. That morning, on the way to her house, I had a weak moment. My insides started shaking, and I decided that rather than quit cold-turkey, I could wean myself off slowly. I had gone all week without it, right? I could just get a little to help me relax and then go four days again. I convinced myself it was a smart plan. I tried to call my dealer to set up a pickup time for that afternoon. After three failed attempts, I pulled into her driveway, and emotion suddenly overcame me. I sat there and cried. She came running out, worried that something was wrong. I asked her if God had the power to interrupt the phone lines. With a puzzled look, she looked at me, then at my phone, and answered, "yes," and at that moment, something broke inside me. I knew God was real, and somehow, he blocked my attempts. He now had my attention.

That night, Matt and I went to dinner and then to the beach to talk. He knew something was up by now because our friends had never watched our kids for us to go out. When we got to the beach, I told him I had something important to tell him, and that we may need counseling to get through it if he still wanted to be with me. There was no easy way to say it. I told him I struggled with addiction, and it had been going on for the last 18 months, and that every time he ever thought I was doing it, he was right. I came clean about every deeply hidden lie that I had. I told him how sorry I was, and this time was different from any of the other times we came to the beach to let things go. I was done and wanted nothing more to do with it.

He was speechless, and oddly, I thought I saw a sigh of relief. He had thought I was going to tell him I cheated on him. After some long, silent moments, he grabbed my hands and said he agreed about needing a counselor.

He said he heard Jesus was a pretty good option, and we should try Him out first. That wasn't what I was expecting to hear. We both dropped to our knees and prayed the best salvation prayer we knew, and we went home and experienced a level of intimacy like no other. That was when I learned the meaning of redemption.

The next morning, we sat down with a calendar to make a plan for friends to step in and help over the next couple of weeks while my body adjusted to the new normal. But I never needed them. I woke up every day feeling normal. No night sweats, inability to function, or depression. My only side effect was I still needed to gain 20 pounds.

Two weeks later, I was finally alone with no one at my door keeping me company in case I had a weak moment. And for the first time in my life, I didn't want it. My desire for the drugs I used to jump hoops to get was finally gone. After 10 long years of addiction, I had been delivered. I sat there in awe and disbelief.

Matt was a true picture of Jesus to me, full of forgiveness, grace, mercy, kindness—all new words added to my vocabulary. He never once shamed or doubted me. My transformation was what he needed to believe that God was real. We dove into church together. I joined the choir and later the worship team. Matt plugged into men's ministry and wherever else he could. We purchased a minivan, got a puppy, and moved houses, all within that first month. I began homeschooling the kids. God lifted our family of five up and propelled us forward to a place we never imagined.

One of my favorite parts about this story is that we weren't even asking for it. We sure didn't deserve it. We weren't living right or doing what we should've been, but God chose to do this amazing work in our lives, anyway. His mercy and grace are for everyone.

Years after we were saved, I heard a teaching on the Passover. I learned it was when God delivered His people from bondage. I am sure that the timing of my own deliverance is no coincidence. Just as each day during Holy Week holds its own significance, the same is true for my story. God made himself known to me each day that week like never before, down to the tiniest detail that the day we accepted Jesus and sealed it was the eighth day of Passover, known as the "Day of New Beginning." If I wasn't the one who experienced these things, I would have a hard time believing it.

## HE WAS ALWAYS THERE...

When God moves in your life, no one can refute it. People will try, but there's nothing more powerful than having an experience with our God. His presence transforms hearts. It's in His presence we find the answers to our greatest struggles. It's in His presence God shows the redeemed and restored you. That's what we experienced those first few worship services but didn't know it. God used those times to soften our spirit and prepare us for His big move. When my desire for drugs disappeared, I had two choices: to press in toward the Lord or turn away and keep using drugs. I was ready for something new. I was tired of hiding, and I learned once I said it out of my mouth, the enemy could no longer lie to me about it. Every time I shared what the Lord had done, I saw people become hungry for their own encounter. God is a God of order. He makes Himself known with dates and numbers. He is in every detail. All we have to do is open our eyes and look.

Have you or someone you know ever struggled with an addiction? It can be a hopeless, desperate feeling; however, I hope my testimony brings you hope that you or your loved one can be free. When I submitted my addiction to the Lord, He did a miracle and took away all my wrong desires. If He did it for me, He can do it for you. Revelations 12:11 says we overcome by the word of our testimony. When is the last time you've shared what the Lord has done in your life?

# 9
## Jesus Changes Everything

*"Therefore if anyone is in Christ, he is a new creation. The old has passed away; behold the new has come."*
- 2 Corinthians 5:17 ESV

Finally, I could see that God had been there throughout it all, from the very beginning, and I wasn't a mistake after all. He did have a plan for me. Everything was different. My likes, dislikes, tastes, smells. Our friends, the music we listened to, and the shows we watched all changed. The empty places within me were disappearing. That thing that I spent my life running away from no longer chased me. The weight that used to crush me had lifted. It felt good every time I confessed another piece of my darkness. There were so many things, Matt once asked me how many things I had left to share, in hopes I was almost done. He was the best during that time, and he experienced his own transformation as well. We were on fire. I reached out to my mom, Gayle, and my siblings, who I had talked with little during those years, to share my newfound freedom in hopes they would want it too, but I soon learned it's all in God's time. I was bummed we had to put our kids back in school because Nick wasn't okay with me homeschooling, but we made the best of it. In hindsight, I wish I fought for homeschooling to avoid some pitfalls that came our way.

Although we lost the friends we had before we got saved, the Lord replaced them with friends who loved Him. He gifted me with some strong, Jesus-loving ladies who discipled me. I learned religion had taught me false beliefs about God and myself, which needed to be dismantled. I have always been an all-or-nothing kind of girl. This was no different. I purchased multiple Bibles in different translations (we didn't have on-line versions like we do today). I loved studying the Word. I had only ever read the King James Version. When I read other versions, the words came alive and filled me with more understanding. I started listening to Joyce Meyer, who said the kind of things I needed to hear, like life is not all about me!

One night, at choir, we were singing the famous song "Amazing Grace." I had sung that handfuls of times throughout my life and never connected to the words until that night. I finally understood the popular phrase, "I once was blind, but now I see." Never before had that made sense to me. For the first time in my life, I could see the goodness of God all around me. I was no longer living just for me. I finally felt like I had purpose.

As the months passed, we found ourselves at church more and more. We served wherever needed. I was eventually asked to join our lead worship team. Reluctantly, I agreed but was not excited about being on stage. We joined our first couple's Bible study, led by the most anointed couple to talk about marriage. We learned so much about what a godly marriage looked like and how to be a blessing to our spouse. We grew leaps and bounds in that class.

God began making himself known in vivid ways. Things happened that made little sense. Accounts we had been paying on, like furniture and appliances, were suddenly paid off. We received untraceable checks in the mail that were always in the amount of an outstanding bill. Matt's previous boss not only helped Matt get his contractor's license, but also gave us his blessing to start our own construction company, and forgave the loan from 2004 of $50,000, which he had given us to start the business we no longer owned. Our faith was growing.

During that time, we were both feeling nudged to grow our family, which was definitely from God because I believed I was done having kids. The desire for more kids felt foreign to me, but we were both learning to hear from God. We had already gotten rid of all our baby things. Dilan was going to be four in a few months. It just didn't make sense. These nudges were strange. We had every reason not to have more kids: finances, house size, etc. Neither one of us could decide what to do, so I just kept taking the pill. In May, we took a trip with a few other families for a week to a beach house. I forgot my pills, and God took His chance. I found out two weeks later that we were expecting.

This pregnancy was different. I still didn't like gaining weight, but I didn't obsess over it like before. When we found out we were having another girl, a friend told me about the name Zoe, and we knew that was it. It meant "life." That is what she brought to our family. She came at the end of January, and I remember saying to Matt how

I could do this again. Who says that right after giving birth? God inspired that. Zoe redeemed everything about pregnancy and babies. She was pure joy. Whereas I used to deal with depression after delivering, all I felt was joy. Since my other three kids were all in school, I had time to just relish with her.

When Zoe was six months old, we moved again to a bigger house in a neighborhood where lots of our friends lived. Months after moving in, we learned the owners were pocketing our rent payment. The bank foreclosed on them, and told us there was no one for us to pay rent to, and that we had a good six to nine months before we needed to leave. It didn't feel right to live there for free. At the same time, money stopped coming in for us because of the economic downfall, and we realized why the Lord had us in that house.

Over the next several months, we began experiencing the hand of God in tangible ways. While I was at a ladies' conference, during worship, I saw my first vision of us leading couples' small groups in our home. I received a prophetic word that my deliverance story would be in a book that would one day transform hearts. Later, after fasting all television shows, we were both given clear details regarding those groups, and the following month, we started our first group. We received our first prophetic prayers in May, and it blew us away. Actually, I thought our friends told the prophets all about us, because there was no way they could know the things they knew. When I realized that didn't happen, I was in awe of God.

2009 was full of signs, wonders, and miracles, where the Lord showed Himself boldly. With little to no money, due to the economic drop of 2008 and some business dealings gone wrong, we learned what it meant to rely on God. Matt learned God was our source rather than him. He always brought home the exact amount of money we needed for the week, with nothing left over. Just as the Lord provided mana for the Israelites while they roamed in the desert, He provided us with the same. At Christmas time, we knew a family who was worse off than us. A friend was taking donations to bless that family. I felt the Lord say, "I'll give you ten-fold whatever you give." We gave $50. Three days later, a couple came to our house and told us God told them to give us a $500 check. We were learning to trust our unseen God like never before.

Our friend group changed again, and this time it hit hard. Through some misunderstandings and false accusations, we had been rejected, my kids included. It was tough because we lived in the same neighborhood, and we felt the rejection and whispers every day. I am wired to want to make things right, to see justice, and this time, I couldn't. I felt wronged and had to learn to stand on Psalm 26:1, which says, "Vindicate me O Lord, for I have walked in my integrity and I have trusted in the Lord without wavering." At the same time, I wished I kept my mouth shut from the beginning. I had to remind myself daily who I was in Christ to battle against what others were saying about me. To keep offense from taking root in my heart, I had to renew my mind daily. It was some of my most lonely months—seven months, to be exact—and then God made His move.

That August, our church had a guest speaker, Mary Forsythe, for our monthly women's meeting. I knew nothing about her, but the day of the meeting, while I was at lunch with Zoe, I was fortunate to meet her because she was having lunch with a friend of mine. We talked a bit, and that was it. That night before the meeting ended, Mary said she had a word for someone and hoped they were in the room. She said, "I met this mom today, and I think her name was Missy or something, but her little girl was Zoe. Is Zoe's mom here?" I was in the front row, and I felt my face flush. This was my second time being called out in a service to receive a prophetic word, so I knew that meant all eyes were on me. Although I was shaking, I stood up, and she walked over to me and asked if she could pray for me. As she prayed, emotion overcame me, and I immediately felt God's presence. There were so many specifics that only He could know. I want to share it here because this word transformed my soul. I did not leave that meeting the same way I entered. I was healed. The questions that haunted me all those nights were finally answered. My faith exponentially grew at that moment. God did see me, and He knew my heart. He had been with me through it all. For the first time that year, I felt peace:

> *The Lord would say, Daughter, it's a time of new rhythm. I'm teaching you that it's the rhythm of the spirit that you must dance to for those that would put demands on you and those that would put expectations on you. And you've had to hold up a shield like never before. For it's a new rhythm, and it's a new dance. And it's a dance with Him. The steps of a righteous man are ordered of the Lord. They're established before you take them. They've already been taken. So the Lord says the next three steps*

*have been well established. They've been well calculated. The rocks have been cut out. They're well placed, but the Lord says they will come at unusually rhythmic times. And when they pop up—it's like you're crossing the pond and your foot is in the air. It's a time of increasing faith. And that's why my timing has been so seemingly sporadic. But I'm gonna connect the dots, and I'm gonna give you revelation of why this was important. For there's a gift of faith that needs to be brought out even from your generations. There's a generational blessing and some faith that some ancestors just didn't fully tap into that I'm making available to you. I'm gonna give you the opportunity to believe, to believe and to believe. But by the middle of April of 2010, the Lord says there will be an establishment of a new level of faith. There'll be three seasons between now and that time. And when that time comes, you will stand with great strength and great courage, daughter. For I've called you as I called Gideon, mighty woman of valor. It is time to come all the way out because I'm calling you in. That's why I've worked so diligently in this past season. In the last seven months, I've been revealing and showing you who you are, helping you combat lies that have tried to captivate your thinking. But it's the dawning of a new day, daughter. It is the dawning of a new day.*

*Father, I thank you for this mighty woman of valor. Father, I thank you for the opening of eyes. Continue, Lord, to show her how you see her. Plant her feet on solid ground. Lord, thank you for her cour-*

*age. It's a force. It's a force. It's gonna be a force. It's gonna be a force. It's gonna be a force. It's gonna be a force. Father, I thank you for the force of courage, rivers of living water, rivers, living, courage, coming out, consuming things that used to deter her. She will overcome. So Father, bless her and her family, Lord.*

*Give Zoe a big hug for me tonight.*

*Bless this family in closing. Amen.*

## HE WAS ALWAYS THERE...

This was our year as baby Christians. Learning to walk in godliness was new and exciting. I never planned on joining the worship team because of fear and unbelief. So when one of the leaders got sick, the Lord used that as an opportunity for me to step in. I resisted my friend that Sunday when she tried to give me a microphone. I couldn't breathe and barely made it through that service. But with each Sunday, I became more comfortable, until I was no longer nervous at all. I'm thankful she saw something in me that I didn't, because leading worship is definitely one of my favorite things.

God used my pregnancy with Zoe to redeem the ones before. The Lord continued to convict us of worldly things we enjoyed that weren't ideal for us. We learned to hear from God in new ways. We learned to look for God in everything. We were hungry for more, and God was faithful to provide the steps for us to walk out, even if they weren't easy ones.

Are fear and unbelief holding you back from stepping into God's plan for your life? Just as God set me free from the bondage of addiction, He also set me free and enabled me to overcome the fear and intimidation controlling my life. First John 4:18 says, "perfect love casts out fear" (ESV). His love set me free from fear, so I could discover things I was created to do and be. He did it for me; He will do it for you, too.

# 10
## Grace Upon Grace

The prophetic word from Mary Forsythe carried me over the next several months. My faith grew continually as our life kept lining up with things said in that word. Once I knew the Lord saw me and was right there with me, it didn't matter what others thought or said. One of our most pivotal, faith-growing moments in our marriage happened a couple weeks after that meeting.

On Friday of Labor Day weekend, in 2009, we experienced the hand of God in a way that changed the trajectory of our family. Zoe was 18 months old, and we were getting back on track from the economic crisis. After all the emotional and financial drama from that year, we decided our family was complete with four kids for many reasons: finances, housing, car size, sanity. After rescheduling his appointment multiple times over the summer, that Friday, Matt had his first "snip snip" appointment. As the weekend approached, I started getting nervous, as I did every time. The night before, I mentioned to Matt maybe we should reschedule again. He was not having it. He was tired of dealing with the fear and anticipation leading up each time, only to delay it. He told me if this wasn't God's desire, He was going to have to make it very clear.

On Friday morning, we sent our four kids out to friends' houses for the long weekend and headed to our appointment. Matt did all the necessary prep work for the surgery: shaving, taking Valium, etc. When we arrived at the office, I filled out the papers, paid the fee, and sat down nervously while Matt drifted off on medications. A couple of hours later, the nurse finally came to us, but she didn't come to call us back for surgery. Instead, she told us that, somehow, they had forgotten to sterilize the equipment, so they wouldn't be able to do his procedure. After a few choice words from Matt, I asked how long that usually took. She said 30-45 minutes. We told her we were happy to wait. Our kids were taken care of, and we're here. She returned about five minutes later and said something we will never forget. Her words exactly: "I am so very sorry, but seeing how it's already 3:30, and it's a holiday weekend, the doctor just doesn't feel like doing any more procedures today, but we can get you back in here first thing Tuesday morning." You can imagine our faces. At that moment, I knew this was the Lord's doing. Who says that? The doctor doesn't feel like it! I took my money back and told them we wouldn't be returning. Matt just kept saying, "I shaved down there for this!" I needed to get him home. I knew, without a doubt, that pregnancy was in my future again.

A couple of weeks later, we found out we were pregnant. It all seemed to make sense. We got chills every time we thought about it. Sadly, a couple of months later, this was our first loss. Then nothing made sense. We didn't understand. We were confused and devastated, but we knew we needed to try again. After months of trying, we finally conceived baby number five in the middle of April—our new establishment of faith from Mary's word. This was the first pregnancy we desired and had to work for. This experience, as traumatic as it was, gave us a new appreciation for life and a true desire to put our family's size in God's hands.

We were pretty sure this time would be a boy because we had already had two girls. Matt was so sure, he told his dad if we had a girl, we would name her Saylor, which was his dad's last name. When the sonogram confirmed she was another girl, I'm sure you can imagine my reaction when I learned he named our baby without asking me. Over time, I came to love the name.

That summer, we found another house to rent, getting us out of that neighborhood. We welcomed Saylor Grace into our home a few days before Christmas. Adding a fifth child was probably our easiest addition. She spent most of her first six months in a car seat while I drove from car line to car line between my kids' four different schools. That was when I knew it was time for me to homeschool. I wanted more time with my kids. I was done wasting time in car lines. I was not happy with the results of public school, and I kept hearing from the Lord that it was up to me to mold their hearts, which can't happen in a couple of hours each day. I took the risk with Nick, willing to fight the matter in court if I had to. But by God's grace, he supported my decision and gave his blessing, and that was the beginning of our new family rhythm. I love how God's ways are higher than ours and that He knows our needs better than we do.

I have so much gratitude to the Lord for stopping our first attempt at finalizing our family. He answered my plea from the night before. I can't imagine missing out on the joy of five more babies. As hard as our first loss was, I can see its fruit. We had two choices. We could get mad, blame God, and turn away, or we could press in and receive God's peace. I have lived enough life apart from God. I know what that's like. One thing I learned is bad stuff happens to everyone. Our response is up to us. We pressed in to God more because of that loss. Regarding my desire to homeschool, I had asked Nick a few times, and every time, the answer was no because his new wife was a schoolteacher. They are sometimes the hardest ones to convince. But over time, God softened their hearts.

Have you turned away from God because of a disappointment or trial? Was there a time when you leaned in rather than pulled away? There is no better time than now to turn back to Him and allow Him to heal your disappointments.

# 11
## Our Greatest Loss

In September 2012, we found out we were expecting baby number six. At just 13 weeks pregnant, we were astounded to see clearly it was our long-awaited boy. We believed this was a fulfilled promise from the Lord. We already knew his name would be Sage. Matt was on cloud nine, and I was thankful, knowing it would be my last pregnancy.

At our 20-week ultrasound, we experienced every parent's worst nightmare. Our baby's heart had multiple defects. And we cried like never before. The next month consisted of lots of doctor appointments, lots of tests and ultrasounds, and a lot of waiting for results. We were relieved to know that there was no sign of any syndrome/chromosome abnormality, but saddened when we received confirmation that there was something wrong with his heart. They transferred our care to Shands in Gainesville, Florida, which is 300 miles from us, where we met with a pediatric cardiologist. After many hours of her just staring at the ultrasound screen and a few appointments, she finally could give us a diagnosis. Sage had Heterotaxy with Right Atrial Isomerism Asplenia Syndrome, along with a few other defects. What a mouthful! She told us most babies with this diagnosis die in utero during the last trimester, and the ones who make it to birth don't have the best chance at surviving. We were told, on more than one occasion, that we would be better off to terminate and start again. We are not the givers and takers of life. That was not an option. I had many thoughts racing through my mind that day, which continued for a couple of weeks. I buried my head in the sand.

Until my revelation. It was a Saturday night, and our pastor and his family came over for dinner. We were watching a memorial service for an 8 year old girl who just lost her battle with cancer, and her dad, who was the pastor, was giving a message. The phrase that got my attention was, "While we want clarity from God, all He wants is our trust." That was exactly right. I wanted God to answer all the questions swarming in my mind, keeping me up all hours. Questions like: How can my baby be sick? I can't stand doctors; how can he be at the doctor all the time? Where will my family be while our baby is having surgery? How can I nurse him if he's in the hospital the first two months of his life? When will I have time to exercise? (I know that's vain, but I'm just being real.) How will we pay for all the medical bills? How can I live in Gainesville without my husband? Where will we live? The questions went on and on. I am a planner, and mostly, I know what's going to happen from day to day or month to month. Having a baby for us was usually just a two-day event and then back to life. So being told all these things was overwhelming. At times, I really wanted to quit all of it. That way, at least, I would be in control and know the outcome. But that phrase changed something inside of me.

I woke up the next morning for church and smiled while I was getting ready. Matt asked me what was wrong or why I was smiling because he hadn't seen that for weeks. I told him about my revelation. I was reminded God was still on the throne. He was not up there looking down, wondering what was going on in the Parenzan home. He was aware and had a plan and a purpose. Regardless of what happens, He would be right here for us. The peace I felt for our situation was the peace that surpasses all understanding. And the cool thing was that Matt had the same peace that morning. He actually said he was excited to see what God would do. I couldn't say I was excited, but I was at peace. I knew we served a God of signs, wonders, and miracles, and when our faith or spirits are down, God is there, holding us up.

Worship music was my main source of encouragement during that time. One of my favorite songs I listened to on repeat during this season was "Give Me Faith" by Elevation Worship. I love the lyrics:

*I need you to soften my heart*
*And break me apart*
*I need you to open my eyes*
*To see that You're shaping my life*
*All I am, I surrender*
*Give me faith to trust what you say*
*That you're good and your love is great*
*I'm broken inside, I give you my life*
*'Cause I may be weak*
*But Your spirit strong in me*
*My flesh may fail*
*My God you never will*[1]

After my revelation, Matt and I lived life like everything was normal. Even though I knew God was on the throne, I had to remind myself daily that, regardless of what happened, we would be okay. Whether that meant we only carried him for 30-something weeks like the doctors said, or had him for a short while, or lived in a hospital for the first year of his life, God would be there to sustain us. Even if I couldn't wrap my mind around it all, I knew He had a purpose. I had a new perspective on what the "peace that surpasses all understanding" meant.

Each time we went to a doctor appointment in Gainesville, we hoped to "Wow!" the doctors, and each time, we were sadly disappointed. We knew God could miraculously heal Sage. We thought it would make for a great story. I'm sure you can imagine how we felt as we neared our due date and the diagnosis was only confirmed, not changed. The one thing we held onto was that he was developing normally, unlike they predicted. So the doctors were puzzled and awed, just not for the reasons we wanted. I didn't understand what God was waiting for, but I trusted He had a plan.

Since we had so many appointments in Gainesville, we wanted to find a church to attend while we were there. Some friends referred us to The Rock of Gainesville. This church was amazing at showing us the love of Jesus. They offered to help us find housing, set up meals while we were there, watch our kids, and more. We felt overwhelmed. Of course, I believed Sage would be healed, and we wouldn't be there long, so we waited on setting any of that up. (Little did we know, Sage would be healed, just not here).

So many people surrounded us with love and support through this crazy time. I don't think we told many people the true extent of his diagnosis because we believed that the doctors were wrong. We loved reading and hearing stories where this was the case. Many people who had lost a child or had a child with a heart defect reached out to share their story with me also, but I didn't want to go there. I didn't want to believe that I might go through that, so I didn't read or listen to those stories.

I think one of the hardest things through this pregnancy was being a mom to the five kids I had at home. Their lives didn't stop. They still needed to be fed, loved, taught, but those were all such hard things to do. Matt and I tried to help them understand our current state of mind without telling them the severity of the situation. Our home was different during those months. I am so thankful for the many friends who took my kids places, or had them over to play, or helped them write papers that I didn't have the energy to do. My kids felt so special during that time. I was so overwhelmed with the amazing group of friends and church families that God surrounded us with to love, support, and build us up, or rather hold us up. Every day, we ran into someone in the community who knew our story and told us they were praying.

Sage's shower was my favorite one. There were over 50 people, full of faith, hope, and expectation of the Lord's plans, who all came to celebrate him. My dear friend June prayed the most beautiful blessing over Sage and me. It was such a special moment. Against most of my friends' wishes, I chose to open all the gifts at home with my four daughters. They had a blast, and I was thankful no one was too upset with me. I have to admit that after we opened everything, Matt and I wondered if we should leave everything in the packaging just in case things didn't work out. We went for it, living in expectation of bringing him home. Sage was alive and kicking, just like any other baby.

It was finally May and time to meet Sage. We scheduled an induction for May 9th to avoid me going into labor on my own. We still hadn't arranged for a place to stay after the birth. I think we both wanted to believe we would take him home. A couple days before induction, we toured the PICU floor, which was something I could've done without. The nurse spoke as if it was a fact that Sage would be on that floor and kept saying how complex and difficult his situation was. We left deflated and exhausted.

On Wednesday, May 8th, we woke up to a call from the hospital asking why we hadn't checked in for our induction scheduled that morning. This surprised us because we thought our plan was to check in that evening to prepare for our 4:00 AM induction the next day. After some communication with our doctors, we confirmed that today was the day. Our emotions were a mess. We got ready and packed up as quickly as we could and headed to the hospital, saying goodbye to the hotel we had stayed for many nights the last couple of months, believing we would not be back.

We arrived at the hospital around noon, checked in, and received a bed. Against my wishes, they hooked up IV fluids and put fetal heart straps across my belly to monitor Sage. It felt like forever waiting for a doctor or someone who knew the plan to come in. For a moment, it was nice because the nurse didn't know of Sage's condition, so it was the first time in a long time that someone spoke to us about him like he was normal. She would say things like, "He looks great on the monitor," or "Wow, such a strong heartbeat." Then when she finally read my chart, which took them hours to find, she was surprised that he looked so healthy on the monitor. She also couldn't believe how "at peace" we appeared. We shared our story with her, and she told us that she didn't come across people like us very often. We were encouraged, for the moment, and thanked God for those He placed in our path.

At 3:00 PM, we wondered how they were going to start an induction and expect him to come at a normal hour. With induction, my body takes its time, like 12 hours from start to finish, with only the last three in labor. That would put his birth in the middle of the night. None of it made sense, and sitting there strapped to the bed with all the fluids going in me was enough to put me over the edge. Finally, the nurse came in and said that the NICU team needed to be available, so induction would begin at 4:00 AM. Yep, another 12 hours away. I insisted to her I needed to get out of there for a while and be unhooked from all the stuff. Another long 45 minutes passed while we waited for her to get approval from the doctor. Given our situation, they allowed it.

Neither of us were hungry, but eating seemed like the only thing to do to pass the time. As we sat at Chuy's, we both broke down for the umpteenth time. The recent events scared and overwhelmed us. It was time to head back to the hospital and prepare for the birth of our baby. When we arrived back in our room, the nurse told us it was a good thing we checked in so early because all the rooms were full, and they would have had to move our induction again. This was another one of God's cool ways of taking care of the details. I am so thankful that He goes before us and prepares the way.

We slept horribly that night in the hospital—me with all my straps and tubes and Matt in one of those chairs that turns into a bed, not to mention the fact that the nurse came in what felt like every five minutes to check vitals.

Finally, around 6:00 AM, the nurse started me on 2 mil/min of Pitocin. Unfortunately, I knew this wouldn't do much, but this was their process. Every 30 minutes, they bumped it up by 2 mil/min. I told the nurse at this rate, I'd be here all day, and that if they'd break my water, it would go a lot quicker. But I was just the patient. By noon, I was up to 20 mil/min, contractions were still bearable, and I was only dilated to 3 cm, which was so abnormal for me. Sage was perfectly happy in there. He had no desire to come into this world. The nurse couldn't believe that I was sitting up talking normally while I had 20 mil/min of Pitocin entering my body. She said this wasn't the norm. I had heard that phrase so many times in my life.

At 12:30 PM, the doctor finally broke my water and upped Pitocin to 22 mil/min. By 1:00 PM, I was dilated to 4 cm and contractions picked up drastically. The next couple of hours are a blur of total pain. Every time I am birthing a baby, I ask myself how in the world I ever made it. Every contraction feels like hours, with no rest in between. I usually cry and sometimes yell. The pain is like no other. But the reward is so sweet. What are a few hours of total and complete hell, right? Matt probably has a different perspective. I am sure he'd like me to get something for the pain. Labor is just as difficult for him in a different way. He sits there helplessly while I endure some of the most difficult moments of my life. He tries, but he is not the best help during those moments.

My body finally overpowered Sage because at 3:17 PM, Sage Matthew entered this world. It was only the second time one of my kids had a doctor in the room at their time of birth. This time, I had about 10 people in the room. It was very strange. They were all waiting for his arrival, waiting to confirm their diagnosis, while Matt and I were waiting for our miracle.

> *"and behold, a voice from heaven said, 'This is my beloved Son, with whom I am well pleased.'"*
> *- Matthew 3:17 ESV*

I only got to hold him for a few moments, just long enough for them to take a picture. I was still pretty out of it, but he looked perfect, just like all the Parenzan babies. I could hardly believe that his insides were messed up. As the NICU team took him away, we prayed harder than we'd ever prayed, pleading with God that they would come storming back in our room with our baby, telling us that somehow everything was normal. That did not happen.

We sat there for what felt like forever, alone in our room, not knowing what to do. This was normally the most joyous moments—holding, feeding, loving on the long-awaited new family addition. But this time, our addition was not with us. It was so strange. We waited. Still, no one came with news.

At 5:00 PM, our cardiologist came in with a report that took our faith to new levels. He confirmed every diagnosis they had previously told us. He said the team wasn't sure how Sage made it this far or how his levels were normal, considering what his insides looked like. But we knew. He said when they gave him the PGE to keep his heart functioning as if in the womb, he stopped breathing, so they had to intubate him. This was disturbing, but they assured us it was normal. He said we could go see him at 6:30 PM and meet with the team to talk about his plan of care. I convinced my doctor to discharge me so I could spend the night with my husband. Given the situation, he allowed it.

Getting dressed and leaving my room a couple of hours after giving birth seemed wrong. It was almost like it had never happened. When we could finally see Sage, neither of us was prepared for what we saw. He was hooked up to all kinds of things. Because he was intubated, we couldn't hear his cry. It was very difficult to keep it together. The nurses were constantly hugging us and telling us how sorry they were.

Nothing could have prepared us for what the surgeon said to us. Sage's detailed diagnosis was a jumble of big words that meant nothing. His mouth was moving in slow motion, and it was hard to understand. He said they had no explanation for why or how Sage was living and breathing in his current state. He said it was necessary for Sage to have surgery immediately and expressed the risks involved with so little time for Sage to acclimate outside the womb. We spent those last few hours with him that evening talking, singing, taking pictures, and praying with him. They made us leave around 10:00 PM.

They said we could come back in the morning at 8:00 to see him off for surgery, so we left to check into our room at the Ronald McDonald House.

Seeing Sage with all the things hooked on him was nothing compared to what he looked like after surgery. That day was the longest day ever, waiting for the doctors to call. What was supposed to be four to six hours turned into eight. Nothing could prepare us for what we saw. His swollen body, chest still open, tiny tubes and chords, all the beeping sounds. It was too much. They said the surgery was a success, and that there was a strength about Sage. They called him the warrior.

The next morning, at 6:00, we headed back to the hospital to be with Sage. We were thankful we hadn't heard from them that night because no news was better than bad news. Seeing his little swollen body with all the tubes and his open wound was still overwhelming. We spent six hours singing and praying and reading the Word to him. It was comforting to see him respond to our voices and our touch. His vitals were doing all the right things.

We were fortunate to have some friends from Destin surprise us with a visit. We could tell that the sight of him was a bit much for them, so we took a break to get some lunch. We hadn't thought about food all morning. Sage was stable and thriving, so we figured an hour away from all the sounds would be good.

I will forever remember our conversation as we sat eating lunch at Chuy's that day. We joked about how Sage couldn't be circumcised and how Matt was going to have to explain that to him one day. We laughed a lot and enjoyed ourselves, considering the circumstances. As I got up to go to the bathroom, I grabbed my purse and noticed multiple missed calls from the hospital. My heart stopped as I listened to the first message—all I heard was Sage needs you. I rushed back to the table in a panic and told Matt to check his phone. He had all the missed calls, too. Our phones were not on silent. How did we both not hear any of the calls, especially when I always hear my phone?

The drive back to the hospital was the longest five minutes ever. The elevator to the top was even longer. As we exited the elevator, I saw the team leaving Sage's room, and I knew. In slow motion, I collapsed on the floor and cried. The next thing I knew, we were in a room with a big table by ourselves, in shock. I know that neither of us expected him to die. We believed with everything in us that God was going to do something big. We would do whatever it took, no matter how hard life would be. We wanted him here with us, as selfish as that sounded.

We were angry. Why did we leave? Why didn't we hear the calls? He fought for his life for 45 minutes. Would it have made a difference if we were there? Those were the questions that haunted our minds and hearts. All the what ifs. Later, we came to the realization that Sage was ready to go, and the Lord, in His infinite mercy, did not let that be our last memory of him.

I don't know how long we sat there, but the doctor finally came in and said we could go see Sage. Walking into that room was rough. We immediately knew it wasn't him. I asked Matt if he wanted to hold him since he never got the chance. But we were both still in shock. We didn't take any pictures or even touch him. I don't know what happened to our friends, but we headed back to our room.

We laid on the bed and cried, not answering any calls, trying to figure out how to share this news. When were we going home? How would we tell our kids? Were we making a mistake not letting them see Sage? Since the next day was Mother's Day, we knew we needed to go home for our kids.

The crying wouldn't stop. The last thing I wanted to do was drive home, but we had five kids at home waiting for us... waiting to meet their brother. No one told them the news because of the gravity of it. That four-hour drive home is what we now call the longest drive ever. I remember when Matt pulled over, right on I-10, to put the empty car seat in the back of his truck, out of sight. We listened to worship music and cried the rest of the way.

When we arrived home, my most vivid memory is of Zoe and Saylor, who were five and two, running to us, excited to see Sage. Zoe was bouncing up and down, looking everywhere for her brother. Matt knelt down to her and said, "Honey, Sage didn't make it. He went to be with Jesus." The blank look on her face, the confusion, then the tears. A few moments later, she asked when his funeral would be. How did she even know what a funeral was? I wanted to retreat to my room. I didn't want to tell the news anymore or talk about the "end of life" things. I didn't want anymore hugs and was so tired of that lump choking me in my throat. As much as I wanted it to all go away, I realized my kids needed closure to losing the brother they never met. With everything inside me fighting against it, we planned his celebration of life ceremony later that week.

We had over 200 people come to support. It was beautiful. I am thankful we got it on video because my memories of that day are few. When I watch the video, it's like seeing it for the first time. Matt spoke words only the Lord Himself could've given him. It is a true picture of what trusting Jesus looks like, even when it's hard:

> *"I didn't think I would be able to do this. When you think about standing in front of a group of people on behalf of your kid, it's normally to celebrate their accomplishments. I got lost in thinking about all the things I could see him doing. I'm going to stick with what he's already accomplished before we even laid eyes on him. He brought us to a place of full submission to God. When we were given his diagnosis, there was absolutely nothing we could personally do to make him better. We had to fully rely on God. We had to fully trust God to do for him what we couldn't do. We thought we had a strong faith and trust in God. Believing for the miracle of healing and life brought us to a whole different level. For starters, our prayer life dramatically increased, and we got real specific. Without ever saying a word, Sage brought a community together to pray and believe in unity for God to perform a miracle. There were people praying from the east coast to the west coast and overseas.*
>
> *Sage brought Misty and I closer to each other. He brought us closer to God than we have ever been. Because of Sage, we are different people. We know what it means to put all your eggs in one basket and believe for big prayers and them not go the way you want. We know what it means to be hurt and still have joy. We will be better parents, better friends, better stewards of the people and things we have*

*been trusted with, better ambassadors of the gospel, and better at seeing people the way God sees them. Sage was only with us for three days. There's only one person I can think of that did more in three days, and that's Jesus. That's not a bad second place. I'm proud of Sage and what he managed to accomplish.*

*I believe Sage would want us to know that our prayers weren't in vain, unheard or unanswered. It couldn't be more opposite than that. If Jesus didn't die and be resurrected, we'd have every reason to be hopeless. But He did, and because He did, we can be full of hope and celebrate the fact that Sage is in Heaven, 100% healed and without blemish. God heard every cry of our hearts and answered every prayer, just not on this side of Heaven or the way that we wanted it. That's okay. God is God. He is good, and He does what He wants to bring Glory to Himself. We want answers, and He just wants our trust. Faith is not just believing there is a God. We have to trust Him. It's because of prayer that he made it as far as he did. They said he wouldn't make it to birth. It's because of your prayers we have the strength to be here today. So, does prayer work? Absolutely.*

*Paul said to mourn with those who mourn and rejoice with those who rejoice.*

*Thank you for mourning with us for the shortness of Sage's life.*

*Even though we are brokenhearted, we ask you to now rejoice with us that He's with Jesus and that his life bared fruit. Look around you...*

*We are so humbled by all of your prayers, love,*

*and support. We couldn't walk this out without you. We love you, Sage loves you, and we thank God for you and thank you for being a tangible picture of Christ to us.*

*Sage Matthew Parenzan*

*Out of all the people in the universe, God chose us. He chose you. There is a void in our souls that may never be filled. Today isn't going to bring us closure, but it's a piece of the puzzle of life. We celebrate you and your accomplishments. We celebrate the gift of life. We give you back to the giver; you were never ours to begin with.*

*Thank you for leaving a mark on our hearts. I'm proud of you. I can't wait to see you again, son. See you soon. I love you."*

So why do I share all this? To give hope to the one who needs it. This day will always bring a little sadness, but I am immediately filled with peace and joy for all that God has done with Sage's life and ours. I didn't think life would ever be the same... and you know what? It's not. It's so much better. God is so good! That's not just a phrase we say.

It is etched in our souls!

## HE WAS ALWAYS THERE...

*"To dance in the midst of terrible suffering is to resolve, 'I will not be a victim. I will not allow this situation to determine the response of my heart, because I have this life, this chance to trust God, to show his reality through my circumstances. I resolve to remain strong and faithful because of the loving God*

> *who holds my hand.'"*[2]
> – Sally Clarkson

Losing a child is the hardest thing I've ever endured. It could have derailed us, but by God's grace, we came out on the other side. At the beginning of every year, I ask the Lord for one word for that year. This year, my word was growth. It is in our deepest sorrows that growth happens. As difficult as this year was, God made Himself known in the tiniest details every day. We learned being specific when we pray mattered. We learned how to renew our minds every time we veered off track. We learned what it meant to really trust God, not just say it. Matt and I would run into strangers who had heard Sage's story and were encouraged by it. Our community rallied around us, provided dinners for over four months, loved on our kids, sent us cards, and more. We learned what it meant for believers to be the hands and feet of Jesus. We learned how to receive.

What have you lost that you had to depend on the Lord to pull you through? Are you still grieving? I don't mean are you still sad about the loss, but rather, has grief taken the joy out of your life? Has it kept you from experiencing the presence of the Lord or gotten you into a place where you are mad at God? Is grief keeping you from looking to the future with expectation? God is truly able to turn your mourning into dancing and to lift your heavy burden if you allow Him to.

# 12
## Our Double Portion

I never could've imagined that one year after saying goodbye to Sage, we would not only be pregnant with another girl, but be adopting a baby boy as well. It is not a situation we went looking for; it fell in our lap.

On my 37th birthday, just seven months after losing Sage, I was finally pregnant again. Every month we tried felt like a year. I didn't care that my doctor advised me to give my body time to heal. I wanted another baby, yesterday. With excitement came fear right behind it. There was no "safe zone" for pregnancy anymore. I battled voices in my mind about all the things that could go wrong and did my best to not check out. I was convinced we were having a boy. The Lord had already given us the name Asher, and that was a boy's name. And why would God give us another girl when he knew how deeply we desired a boy?

Then in January, we had a missionary family over for dinner who had four daughters. As the dad was talking, he introduced his family, and one of his daughter's names was Asher. I looked at Matt and shook my head. There was no way Asher could be a girl's name. Doubts started looming.

At the end of February, a friend called to ask me if I knew of any shelters that accepted kids. She knew a young mom six-months pregnant, with a five-year-old, about to be evicted from her home because of dire circumstances. I was annoyed she called me. But I felt led to mention it to Matt. This was out of character for me because, sadly, I wouldn't often allow things into my life that would disrupt my plan. That I was still thinking about this girl caught my attention. After talking with Matt, we decided the first thing I should do was call and talk to her to be sure she wasn't involved with drugs or alcohol or other toxic things we should avoid. During that conversation, I was open with Becca and told her I called her because I felt like the Lord told me to. She seemed sweet, so I invited her and her daughter Shavaya, as well as my friend Kim, over for dinner the next night.

Once we finished eating, all the kids ran off. That left Matt and I with Kim and Becca. As we were talking, I heard the words, "Pregnant with a son, looking for a family and God's promise." Startled, I looked behind me. Matt gave me the questioning look of, "are you okay?" No. I was confused. I was already pregnant with my son. Why would I need another one? I couldn't keep quiet, so I asked Becca if she was having a boy and looking for a family. She looked at my friend like she told me something she wasn't supposed to. I reassured her that Kim said nothing, and that I just had a feeling. I was trying not to show my shock at the realization of what this meant. Our ultrasound appointment would be the next day. I was no longer sure of anything.

We followed our doctor into the ultrasound room. At all the appointments leading up to this one, we were so sure we were having a boy. My doctor had been through a lot with us, so she didn't want to miss being there when we found out. She noticed our lack of excitement and asked if everything was okay. I told her to just hurry and check, and then I would tell her what was up. In minutes, she confirmed it. We were having another girl. I love how God let us in on His plans the day before our appointment, so we wouldn't be quite as shocked.

After telling my doctor the whole story, she wasn't surprised. She said with us, anything is possible. We set Becca up as her patient and scheduled all our future appointments together. Becca and Shavaya moved in with us that weekend. As news got out, we were flooded with all kinds of responses, good and bad. We were called selfish for adopting a baby when we were already pregnant. One couple, who had been trying to adopt for a while, came to us and said the Lord told them we were supposed to allow them to adopt the baby. People judged us for moving them in our house. Others were worried that she would change her mind during the 48-hour waiting period after birth, and they wanted us to be worried as well. My perspective was if she changed her mind in those two days, then we would give her the support necessary, because I was already having a baby. If the Lord wanted us to have her baby, then He would make it happen. I was thankful for our small band of support that stood by us and held us up during that time. We found Becca a job close by, and her daughter mixed right in with our daily homeschool fun. They attended church with us each week as well. They became part of our family.

The adoption process was more intense than we expected. In my mind, if someone is pregnant, and they choose a family to adopt, it should be simple. Not a chance. We had to go through the same process and pay the same amount as anyone adopting a baby. It took me talking to four different counselors to find one who would even approve us with the amount of kids we already had. In fact, the first person I talked to told me he'd never approve us because he didn't believe kids in big families got as much love as those in smaller ones. I asked him how many siblings he had. It turns out he only had one. I then asked if this was his opinion or Florida Law. He told me it was his professional opinion. I knew this was God's will, so I hung up and tried another. God was with us through it all.

In April, I flew to California to see my siblings and my birth mom for the first time in ten years. I felt nervous and excited. So much had happened for all of us in that time. Caanan and Brittany were all grown up. The similarities between me and my sister were more obvious now that we were adults. They all thought I was nuts when I told them things going on in my life. But I learned that there's something special about siblings; it doesn't matter how much time passes, we can pick right back up.

The reality that we were going to have two babies was growing each day. We knew we needed to come up with a boy name since we already knew our girl would be Asher Bella, from the verse Isaiah 61:3, which says He makes beauty out of ashes. That night in bed, I suggested Isaiah, and Matt got so excited, saying how great it would be to call him Izzy for short. I shot him down immediately.

That was a girl's name to me, and I just didn't like it. Then he looked up the meaning and laughed. He told me I would change my mind once I knew the meaning, and he was right. In Hebrew, Izzy means God's promise, which is what the Lord had already called that baby. So that night, we went to bed knowing our babies would be called Asher Bella and Isaiah (Izzy) Matthew.

June came, and Izzy was born on June 5th. This was my first time being on the other side of labor, and it was definitely different. Matt and I were in the room with Becca during her labor. Matt left when it was time to push, but I stayed with her and was part of the whole experience. Izzy came out smiling. He looked so much like a Parenzan. The Lord made sure we knew He was right there with us. Becca did great. I held him first, but then handed him to her. I know that the decision to give him up was the hardest, most selfless one she had ever made. She wanted Izzy to have a father and couldn't provide that to him. She signed the papers after the allotted time. Once they were discharged, we returned home.

Becca continued living with us for the next few months while she recovered. I couldn't have done what she did. She never over stepped or made things awkward. People would ask how much longer she was going to live with us. And we would tell them our goal was never to just take her baby and kick her out. We wanted to set her up in a way that she would not find herself back in the same situation. She moved out the week Asher was born in August. We were sad to see them leave but knew it was time.

We continued our relationship with them. Our situation was not the norm. To this day, eight years later, we still see them often, and Izzy knows he was in Becca's belly, not mine. We knew it was important for him to know the truth, considering what the lie my parents told me did to my life.

During this time, our teens struggled severely. They both acted out in many ways. I did not handle their misbehavior well at all. I was angry and felt like they were being selfish. I was too caught up in my own grief to recognize acting out was their way of dealing with grief. I didn't realize how the loss of Sage and their grandpa had affected them until years later.

It finally got so difficult, we sent Travis to a program called Teen Challenge, about six hours away from us. To this day, he has not forgiven us for this. He called me around day 60, which was June 5th, Izzy's birthday, and asked if he could come home. I said no. I didn't feel like anything would be different. He checked himself out of the program and made his way back to Destin. He moved in with his grandma (my adoptive mom), which turned out to be an unhealthy refuge. She was always clueless to my doings when I was young, and she hadn't changed. We saw him a few times and tried to mend our relationship, but the rantings about me from his grandma had too much power. We are still believing and praying for the return of this son.

The goodness of God in blessing us with two babies overwhelmed us. I never had adoption in my plan, but I am grateful God made it happen. We were fortunate to see the hand of God move in very tangible ways daily. We referred to Izzy and Asher as our providential twins because God's providence brought them together.

Life with two babies was nothing like I imagined. It wasn't 1 x 2 but rather 1 x 100. So after 13 years in Destin, we finally moved to Santa Rosa Beach to see Matt more. I needed help and was finally willing to move. Leaving everything I knew to be home, I chose to trust that the Lord would be with us through it all.

HE WAS ALWAYS THERE...

Although I am adopted, adoption was never part of my plan. God was all over this. When my friend texted me, all I could think was, "Doesn't she know what my life is like right now?" I was three months pregnant with baby number seven, still grieving the loss of Sage from nine months earlier, and a mom to my five kids at home. But she did know. She also knew God told her to reach out to me, and whether I wanted to or not, He then kept at it until I conceded. I could've kept on with what I was doing and not given it another thought, but by now, I had learned what a God-nudge felt like. When things don't make sense, the Lord is usually up to something.

I also learned that with obedience comes blessings. I never imagined the outcome of that decision to make that call. Hearing His voice at the kitchen table that night is a memory I will never forget. He was with us every step of the way, even when we felt alone. It was always the Lord's plan for Izzy to be part of our family. I love that we still have a relationship with his birth mom because I know how important that will be to him one day. These types of relationships are rare without God in the midst.

Losing my oldest son to the world is still one of my deepest hurts, but I have finally found a peace that only

God can provide. Where I used to be filled with regret for my early parenting days, the time and space have allowed me to focus more on parenting my other children differently, as well as prepare my heart to be gracious and forgiving when he returns. I have been through all the stages of loss with him and will continue to stand on Proverbs 22:6 that says, "train up a child in the way he should go and when he is old he will not depart from it." This verse gives me hope. I also know it is in God's time and not mine. If you're experiencing the loss of a prodigal child who isn't currently in touch with you, you probably feel helpless. But our God is a God of compassion and hope, who loves our children more than we do. Give yourself permission to grieve.

Do you have a prodigal or an estranged family member? Are you in contact with him/her? Do you feel helpless or hopeful? Have you allowed yourself time to grieve? Have you forgiven yourself for their departure? Continue to pray for them because God is faithful to hear our prayers.

## 13
## And the Journey Continues

Life normalized as Izzy and Asher got older. We could participate in things again. I had lost most of the baby weight I gained with Asher and was feeling more like myself. In November, we took our first trip away from the kids to Mexico for Matt to officiate my sister's wedding. I loved the new freedoms we had.

December 9th, 2015, was another memorable evening. The next day, Matt was scheduled for his "snip snip" appointment, this time for real. Our providential twins were 16 and 18 months old, and I was finally seeing a glimpse of light. That night, my wonderful hubby asked me if we could try one more time for a boy. He explained how great it would be for Izzy to have a brother. Oh, that was a heavy blow! I was done having kids, and everyone knew it. I was tired and not ready to be pregnant again, and was definitely good with my five girls. But I couldn't discount his desire, so I came up with a plan—yep, a Misty plan—to guarantee we would have a boy. I gathered all my goodies and info and tried to wrap my head around doing it again. We would start trying in April, because good things always happened during that month, and the

Chinese calendar said a boy (although now I realize not to give any credence to that). I wasn't taking any chances with this one. I was going to be 40 in a few days, so this would absolutely be my last pregnancy!

As usual, God had other plans. We found out on Christmas Day, just two weeks later, we were expecting. God wasted no time!

I was so thankful the Lord, in His mercy, waited until I had a change of heart before blessing me with another baby because until that time, I was unwilling to be pregnant again. I was a bit stunned that Christmas, though not entirely. The Lord has a sense of humor and always wants me to know that it's Him, not me. We didn't tell anyone our news. People's responses to hearing about a ninth pregnancy are extreme. We waited until we could confirm it was a boy, while preparing for the possibility of it being a girl. But by the end of January, my belly had popped out enough for my girls to notice. A couple of weeks later, a blood test confirmed we were having a boy. Everyone was excited. So here I was, 40 years old, having my last baby.

Pregnancy number nine was, by far, my easiest. I was pretty sure it was the new supplements I had been taking, but I was thankful, especially considering I had two littles not quite two years old yet. I was thankful we made the move to Santa Rosa Beach the previous summer. We lost so much time in Matt's commute each day that moving closer was one of our best decisions.

Bryana struggled. She had it in her head that when she turned 18, she could quit school and move in with grandma, just like Travis did. This thinking caused her to withdraw emotionally and disengage from all things family. We lost another one to the unhealthy refuge. This was tough on my heart, and I admit, I probably didn't handle it in the best way.

We named our last baby Zane, which in Hebrew means God is gracious. Boy, does that fit him well. All our boys had the middle name Matthew, so I assumed that would be his middle name, but Matt had other ideas. He wanted Zane to have the initials ZAP, so he said since he was due in August, we should make that his middle name. I thought that was the silliest thing I'd heard, but we took a vote at our couple's baby shower, and to my surprise, August won.

Adding Zane brought with it lots of changes. We needed a bigger family vehicle. I cried. I loved our minivan, and I didn't want to drive a big church bus. I had to get over it, though. It actually wasn't as bad as I imagined, and now I love our bus. Our house already felt small, but now the 2400 square feet felt like a mere thousand.

Having three kids two-years-old and under was one of my most difficult parenting seasons. Attending church was a struggle. It also meant very little homeschooling would happen, so I put Zoe and Saylor in a local Christian school, Izzy and Asher in a nearby preschool, and enrolled Dilan and Bryana in online classes. It was one of our worst homeschool years. Bryana moved in with her grandma that following June after her 18th birthday, dropped out of school, and eventually cut off relationship from us for a long time. If I could do that year over, we would've had a grace year and focused on relationships, family time, and read-alouds (we love reading books aloud together). Ultimately, those are the things that matter. Unfortunately, it's taken me all these years to realize the things that make the real difference.

Zane brought everything full circle. I could look back on our journey of having babies and clearly see the Lord's hand along the way. Had he given us a boy earlier, we would've missed out on so much. Zane is a "mini-me" to his dad. I always said I wanted a little brown boy like his dad. I got just that. God is good all the time. Our family was now complete, for real this time.

HE WAS ALWAYS THERE...

God has such a sense of humor. Over the years, I have learned to just laugh out loud. I wasn't laughing when I became pregnant so soon, without incorporating my plan! He did it in such a way that I couldn't even look at the Chinese calendar, which I know isn't dependable, but it had been right for all my kids, so for this last pregnancy, I was going to use it to pick the month for us to try. I got pregnant on my birthday weekend, and the calendar said we would have a girl if we conceived before my birthday or a boy if it was after. That detail I didn't know because it could've been any of those nights. I knew He did that on purpose just to show me He was greater than any calendar!

Have you experienced God's sense of humor? How has He surprised you with His blessings? Have you learned to trust that His ways are higher than your ways?

# Epilogue

*"And we know that for those who love God
all things work together for good, for those who
are called according to his purpose."*
– Romans 8:28

Here we are in 2023. Our life is full of ups and downs, twists and turns, with the Lord by our side. From the time Matt and I met, I pictured us sitting in rocking chairs on our front porch, watching our tribe of grandchildren run and play in the yard. I envisioned the 30-foot-long table at Thanksgiving, followed by the family picture of fifty-plus people, all stemming from us. And while we aren't in the season of rocking chairs or the 30-foot table yet, we are moving toward the fifty-plus. We have had to pioneer our own way by taking risks and teaching our kids to do hard things. Because we were both raised on rocky ground, we have had to build our own foundation to raise our family on. We have spent the last decade fixing the cracks and sinkholes from our first decade, and while we are still walking out the consequences of those actions, we are better for it. I love that the Lord has given us an extra opportunity, or rather a second chance, at parenting. We made so many mistakes in those first ten years, but we learned so much! I love our second family, as we call it, and I love even more that Bryana and Dilan are still around to see what a healthy family looks like. I have watched the Lord redeem every one of my messes for His glory. I am confident it wasn't all for nothing. He makes all things work together for good.

Our life is beautiful. We currently live on ten acres in our forever home that Matt built. His parents, Lola and Pop, as well as Auntie, who had lived in Crestview for fourteen years, live in their forever home on the same property. Our kids run "across the way," as we say, each morning at 7:00 AM for hot chocolate and Nutella toast. They help Lola in the garden and the kitchen. Pop takes them fishing, on walks, to the park, to the gas station, and wherever else their little hearts desire. Dinner on any given day includes 12-15 mouths to feed. I'm soaking in what may be our last season with all but one of our children living at home.

Travis is 26 and is still searching for his way in life. He is intelligent and funny, and I bet he still loves music. He blessed us with a granddaughter, Myla, five years ago. We waited and prayed and waited and prayed to meet that little girl. After over two years, that day came, not with Travis, but with her mom, Cami. I am thankful she invited us into her life and fully believe God had something to do with that. She is now married and has another little girl. We try to have them over weekly for dinner. We love them like family. I love how the Lord has blessed that relationship. Although we haven't seen

Travis for eight years, we get something wonderful as we wait—his daughter, who has all of his good qualities. We are praying for his return.

Bryana is 23 and has come and gone a handful of times over the years until she returned home last year with a baby. Every detail of her return had God stamped all over it, and I hope to one day be able to share the story with her. Luka just turned one, and the two of them live with us. She is a good mom. She has come so far in such a short time. I love that we get to do life together again. They attend church with us and participate with the family, but she is still finding her way. She is walking a very similar path I walked, but does not see it. She is beautiful, witty, and funny. We pray each night for her to experience the Lord the way only He knows she needs Him.

Dilan is 19 and recently returned from Word of Life Bible Institute, where she spent two years studying the Bible. She brought her prospective mate Ethan back with her. We absolutely love him. She sleeps in Lola and Pop's guest room because Ethan sleeps in ours to avoid being under the same roof before marriage. She is still our free-spirited dreamer, who loves the Lord deeply. She has a level of compassion and empathy that I admire and is beautiful inside and out. She brightens every room she enters. The favor and anointing of God follows her wherever she goes.

Zoe, our old soul, is almost 15 (I'm not allowed to say she is 14 anymore). She is my first daughter to pass me in height. Her beauty is stunning. Up until a few months ago, she was the oldest in the house for the two years that Dilan was gone, and she rocked it. She is our compliant peacemaker (our only one), who is always the first to give up her want for others with a smile. If I could change her middle name, I'd make it Joy because she brings joy to everyone she meets. She has a servant's heart and loves others like Jesus.

Saylor is 12 and is our logical brainiac. This girl impresses all of us daily. She makes homeschooling look easy. Whatever she does, she does with intensity. She leads with a strength that she is still learning to manage. Her voice carries the breath of God that will transform hearts. There is an anointing on her that she hasn't embraced yet. She will one day have the boldness to do miracles.

Izzy is 8. He is our tender one, with a smile that melts your heart and a personality to match. He loves to build legos and play with friends. He is currently on his fourth time reading through his children's Bible by choice. He is a deep thinker who likes to be pursued. His love for the Lord is evident. Volunteering at church is his new favorite thing.

Asher is 8, and she wins the prize for asking the most questions. This girl has always been inquisitive about everything! She is our spunky fireball. It is next to impossible to convince her to do something she doesn't want to, a lot like her mama. She is artistic and funny. I love that she still wants to dress like me. Her independence challenges me and continues to remind me God has a plan for each of my kids.

Lastly, Zane, who is 6, continues to refine me daily. Unaware of his strength, his hugs are as hard as his punch. He is all things fast and hard. He is rough, tough, driven, and independent and not easily persuaded. He has the biggest heart and a smile as bright as the sun. He is his daddy's clone, who has caused me to question everything

I thought I knew about parenting. He leads with a strength and confidence that could only come from the Lord.

*The Parenzan Family*

We love our church. Our kids love our church. We are coming up on our two-year mark at Vision Church, and many days, I ask the Lord why we had to wait so long to try it. He continues to remind me we wouldn't have been ready any earlier. His timing is always best and rarely in line with our timing. But I am thankful God's ways are higher than mine. I now get to witness my kids grow their own faith. I see them lift their hands in worship and pray fervently for His will. I have never been surrounded by so many people who genuinely love the Lord and live the same every day as they do on Sunday. In the past couple of years, I have taught myself how to play the piano and have written many Psalms to song as well as a few original songs. It can only be God, because there is no other explanation.

Matt is a great man of God who lives his life with integrity and excellence in all areas. He is passionate about encouraging men to be better husbands, fathers, and friends. He leads a men's weekly prayer group, rain or shine, ranging from 20 to 30 guys, all desiring to grow deeper in the Lord. He is a family man, for sure. He runs a successful construction company with a partner whom God blessed us with almost 15 years ago. We don't just do business with our partners, but we get to do life as well. We are full of gratitude and give all credit to the Lord.

Most days, I do not feel like I deserve the life the Lord has blessed me with, but that's the best part. None of us deserves it, and that's why we need His gift of mercy and grace. Matt and I just celebrated our 20th wedding anniversary. We are in our best season yet. We always tell people, on a scale from 1 to 10, our marriage is a 20. I know this is because we are intentional in keeping Jesus in the center. We've had a handful of seasons when that wasn't the case, and we suffered because of it. I love that the Lord continues to use us as a couple to encourage others.

When people ask me how we do it, I honestly don't know how to answer it. Saying "by God's grace" doesn't satisfy them, but that is the only explanation. I feel like God blinded us through the process to complete His plan because I'm not sure we would have gone along with it. The Lord continues to speak loudly in our lives, and we do our best to obey what He says, even if it's not what the majority are doing. I lived on the world's path for more than half of my life. I know where that leads.

If you got this far, then I applaud you. I challenge you to look back over your life and see all the areas God has blessed you. Write those things down. Make a list of all the things you are grateful for. Make a list of all the areas you'd like to see growth, and then pray over them and ask the Lord to help you. I've included a 30-day devotional with some of my favorite Bible passages for you to meditate on to get to know our Savior.

Lastly, always remember, He is always there.

# 30 Days to a New You

THE SERENITY PRAYER

*God grant me the serenity
To accept the things I cannot change;
Courage to change the things I can;
And wisdom to know the difference.*

*Living one day at a time;
Enjoying one moment at a time;
Accepting hardships as the pathway to peace;
Taking, as He did, this sinful world
As it is, not as I would have it;
Trusting that He will make all things right
If I surrender to His Will;
So that I may be reasonably happy in this life
And supremely happy with Him
Forever and ever in the next.
Amen*[3].

## PRAYER OF SALVATION

Do you know Jesus as your Savior? Would you like to have a relationship with Him? If you do, you can start today by committing and submitting your life to Him. It starts with a simple, heartfelt prayer:

God, I recognize that I have not lived my life for you until now. I have been living for myself, and that is wrong. I need you in my life; I want you in my life. I acknowledge the completed work of your son, Jesus Christ, in giving His life for me on the cross at Calvary, and I long to receive the forgiveness you have made freely available to me through this sacrifice. Come into my life now, Lord. Take up residence in my heart, and be my king, my Lord, and my Savior. Please send your Holy Spirit to help me obey you. From this day forward, sin and the desire to please myself will no longer control me, but I will follow you all the days of my life. Those days are in your hands. I ask this in Jesus' precious and holy name. Amen.

As you know, my walk with the Lord has been a journey. I did not become who I am today over night. I had to be intentional with my words, thoughts, and actions. The Bible is full of life. This is a collection of some of my favorite verses. They gave me hope when I needed it and still do. I have included a short prayer with each one in hopes of deepening your relationship with our Savior. My prayer for you is as you read, ponder, and pray over these verses for the next 30 days, your faith will grow as well as the knowledge of who God is and whom He has created you to be.

# Day 1

*"Therefore, if anyone is in Christ, he is a new creation. The old has passed away; behold, the new has come."*
– 2 Corinthians 5:17 ESV

Years ago, one of my favorite TV series was The Biggest Loser. There was something magical about watching people change their lives by transforming their bodies. Having been pregnant nine times, I can assure you the process itself is not magical. It is tedious and tiresome. It took determination and discipline. But the results were always worth it. I think these transformation shows drew me because they reflect the very work that God longs to do in each of our hearts and lives.

This is the first verse that came to life right in front of me. When I received Christ as my Savior, He exchanged my old life for a new one. I exchanged sin for forgiveness, pride for humility, legalism for grace, fear for love, weakness for strength, and anger for joy. No one knew more than me the extent of my transformation. Day by day, God stripped off my old habits and thoughts that kept me blind and replaced them with His truth. I had to surrender every area of my life and live in obedience to His will. It was a daily battle, but the newfound joy and peace I felt made it all worth it.

*Jesus, I thank you for making me a new creation in you. Your life is now mine, and my old ways are no more. May the boasting of my weakness show the world that you are Lord of my life and more powerful that my past, present, or future. Amen.*

# Day 2

*"Finally, brothers, whatever is true, whatever is honorable, whatever is just, whatever is pure, whatever is lovely, whatever is commendable, if there is any excellence, if there is anything worthy of praise, think about these things."*
- Philippians 4:8 ESV

One of the most helpful things I have learned since walking with the Lord is that all sin begins in our thoughts. It's in our thinking that we make plans good or bad. If we want to grow in godliness, we must win the battle over sin on the thought level.

This verse is a constant reminder to keep my thoughts in check. When you dwell on all the blessings, the character of our loving God and Father, and all His beauty seen in nature, then you can more easily live from those settling truths. However, whenever you think about what you don't have and what is wrong with the world, you will struggle with depression and anxiety. The mind is a battlefield. Life will always move in the direction of your strongest thoughts.

*Righteous and Holy God, you are marvelous and glorious, perfect in every way, and beyond my comprehension. Keep me from destructive thoughts. Fill my mind with your goodness. Please help me see and focus upon the good and glorious things you place in my path today. Amen.*

# Day 3

*"No temptation has overtaken you that is not common to man. God is faithful, and he will not let you be tempted beyond your ability, but with the temptation he will also provide the way of escape, that you may be able to endure it."*
– 1 Corinthians 10:13 ESV

This is one of the most misquoted verses. The key point isn't in the part saying He won't give you more than you can bear. The key point is that He will provide a way out, so that you can endure it. We can do all things in Christ who gives us strength. We will be tempted, tested, and tried, but we are given a way to endure it, and that way was born to us in a manger (Jesus). Invite Jesus into your life—make Him the main character. Read scripture. In doing this, you will gain wisdom and strength to endure the many trials of this world.

*Lord, thank you for providing a way of escape from temptation. Sustain me and make me stronger, so I will have the power to face it victoriously. Help me make better decisions. Help me focus on things that matter. Help me to follow you with holiness, hope, and faith! Amen.*

# Day 4

*"O Lord, you are my God; I will exalt you; I will give thanks to your name; for you have worked wonders, plans formed long ago with perfect faithfulness."*
- Isaiah 25:1 NASB

Matt and I have experienced so many signs and wonders throughout our walk with the Lord. I learned early on to write things down to reflect on later. At the end of 2009, the year the economy bottomed out, Matt expressed his disappointment for that year. Then I brought out the list, and he was reminded.

We encourage our kids to keep a gratitude journal because the enemy wants us to forget the things God has done. Praise is our weapon that silences the enemy and gives us strength. It creates an atmosphere for the Holy Spirit to work and for God to answer prayers.

Perhaps you feel there's nothing to praise God for. That's okay. I've been there too. The important thing is to realize when you're at your lowest, praise can be most powerful.

So today, take some time to praise God. It doesn't have to be a long thing. A minute or two will do. But remember God's goodness. Remember the good things He has done and how much He loves you!

*Dear Heavenly Father, you are my God, my Lord, and my salvation. I will praise your name forever and ever, for you have done wonderful things for me and for all who trust in your unfailing goodness and mercy. Praise the Lord, oh my soul, and let all that is within me glorify and worship His holy name. Amen.*

# Day 5

*"You will keep in perfect peace....*
*All whose thoughts are fixed on you, whose minds*
*are steadfast, because they trust in you."*
*- Isaiah 26:3*

The times when I tend to lose my peace are when I take my focus off Jesus, or rather, my relationship with Him goes idle. Holidays are times set aside to celebrate something special. But with most celebrations comes an additional list of to-dos. December is one of our busiest months, no matter how hard I try to simplify it. I've learned that, with the numbers I'm working with, simplicity is a challenge. If I am not intentional, the first thing to go are my quiet moments with Him throughout the day. It's in these moments, He gives me what I need for the day. His peace matters! His presence changes the atmosphere.

*Lord, in your presence is where I find joy. In my moments of worry, help me remember your good nature and the hope you offer. As I go about my day, fill me with your perfect peace, no matter what I face. In Jesus' name, Amen.*

# Day 6

*"Let the words of my mouth and the meditation of my heart be acceptable in your sight, O Lord, my rock and my redeemer."*
- Psalm 19:14 ESV

As much as I try (and fail), this remains one of my core life desires—that my thoughts, words, and actions bring pleasure and glory to Jesus. Easier said than done, right? I never realized how much my thoughts determine my actions. If what we watch and listen to affects our thoughts, then we need to be mindful of those things. When God delivered me from my addiction, my pastor's wife told me the most important thing for me over those first few months was to remove all secular movies, music, books, and the like from my life, and replace them with wholesome things. This made all the difference. I love these two quotes: "All transgressions begin with sinful thinking" (Billy Graham[4]); "Wrong thinking leads to wrong feelings, and before long the heart and mind are pulled apart and we are strangled by worry. We must realize that thoughts are real and powerful, even though they cannot be seen, weighed, or measured" (Warren Wiersbe[5]).

*Dear God, I thank you that I filter all my thoughts through your Word, so I can think rightly about myself. I will know the Word so well, I can detect all the thoughts from the enemy of my soul. Let my words and actions praise you. Guide my lips so I utter no evil. I will embrace your Word and rest in your strength. Amen.*

# Day 7

*"When you pass through the waters, I will be with you; and through the rivers, they shall not overwhelm you; when you walk through fire you shall not be burned, and the flame shall not consume you."*
– Isaiah 25:2 ESV

For a huge portion of my life, I was unaware God was there. But He was always there, walking by my side. He never let the waters of adversity overwhelm me. He never let the fiery trials burn and consume me.

We often cannot see the way out when we're in the midst of the storm. This is why we need to keep close to God. There is purpose in everything God does. No experience, emotion, or trial goes wasted. He is working good on our behalf. So when I feel this way, I remember the promise that God is with us, and He is working even when we can't see Him.

*Dear Jesus, thank you for always being with us. I know that sometimes I am unaware of your nearness or of your providence at work throughout my life. In those times, dear God, please give me confidence and perseverance to stand through the times of trial so that I can also share in your times of triumph. Amen.*

# Day 8

*"The Lord is my shepherd; I shall not want. He makes me lie down in green pastures. He leads me beside still waters. He restores my soul. He leads me in paths of righteousness for his name's sake. Even though I walk through the valley of the shadow of death, I will fear no evil, for you are with me; your rod and your staff, they comfort me. You prepare a table before me in the presence of my enemies; you anoint my head with oil; my cup overflows. Surely goodness and mercy shall follow me all the days of my life, and I shall dwell in the house of the Lord forever."*
- Psalm 23 ESV

In our world, it's so easy to get stressed out and weary. It seems like something always demands our attention, and the fast-paced demands of everyday life can be overwhelming. God doesn't want us to live overwhelmed. Instead, we can live in God's rest and have a much more peaceful and joyful life. I love Psalm 23 because it comforts and encourages me to find renewal in God's presence by following His lead. The key to being at peace and finding the rest we need is trusting and following God's guidance in every area, even when it's hard. Making choices using God's wisdom will keep us on the right path. God is always good, and He always wants what's best for us. As we learn to trust him completely in all things, we will experience more peace and rest, no matter our circumstances.

*Lord, forgive me when I look to the things of this world for refreshment. It is only in you I will find rest. You are my source of strength and protection. Nothing I go through is unseen or wasted. I will fear no evil, for you are with me. Amen.*

# Day 9

*"Stop imitating the ideals and opinions of the culture around you, but be inwardly transformed by the Holy Spirit through a total reformation of how you think. This will empower you to discern God's will as you live a beautiful life, satisfying and perfect in his eyes."*
- Romans 12:2 TPT

Mindset is everything! What you think about, you bring about. If you allow negative thoughts to shape your mind, your life will lack peace, joy, and hope. As a mom of nine kids, my days are full. I have little downtime. Each morning, I do my quiet time, a workout, and a shower, then my day doesn't stop until my head hits the pillow. My days are filled with schooling, laundry, grocery shopping, meal planning, rehearsals, play dates, cooking, dental exams, and the list goes on. I have had seasons when my head gets in the way, and I get overwhelmed thinking about all the things that won't get done if I stop to rest. Those heavy thoughts bring depression, and everything begins to feel like a chore. That thinking brings no joy to me or my family. I had to learn to reject those burdens by choosing gratitude. Gratitude is a game changer. Rather than starting my day saying, "I have to do this or that," I keep joy alive when I change it to, "I get to do this or that." It makes all the difference. People say "change your thoughts, change your life." It's true!

    *Lord, I long to break free from negative thinking and embrace peace, joy, and optimism. I invite you to transform my thought patterns and help me recognize, reject, and replace thoughts that are not pleasing to you. Amen.*

# Day 10

*"My fellow believers, when it seems as though you are facing nothing but difficulties, see it as an invaluable opportunity to experience the greatest joy that you can! For you know that when your faith is tested it stirs up in you the power of endurance. And then as your endurance grows even stronger, it will release perfection into every part of your being until there is nothing missing and nothing lacking."*
- James 1:2-4 TPT

Tests, trials, hardships, and pains do not come in order to frustrate us, but to challenge us to remain steadfast. When I look back over my life, I am in awe of what the Lord has done and continues to do. Life with Jesus hasn't been easy by any means. He never said it would be easy, but He did say it would be worth it, and I agree. With every trial or disappointment, my faith grows, and my spirit is strengthened. Suffering is painful, but it is vital to growing in godliness. There is joy beyond all suffering to focus on. We must persevere and remind one another of that hope.

*Dear Lord, help me count it all joy when trials or disappointments come my way. Give me the strength, patience, knowledge, understanding, and courage I need to conquer my storms. I put my trust in you. Help me seek you, always. Amen.*

# Day 11

*"And the Lord will guide you continually and satisfy your desire in scorched places and make your bones strong; and you shall be like a watered garden, like a spring of water, whose waters do not fail."*
– Isaiah 58:11 ESV

This verse makes itself most evident in my life with my family size. I remember when we only had three kids. We ate lots of grilled cheese and ramen noodles, macaroni and cheese with hot dogs, spaghetti and yes, God help me, even Hamburger Helper. We also did a weekly paper route for $65 each week, which is what we used to buy our food. My point is when we gave our lives to Jesus in 2006, we felt like the Lord wanted us to trust Him with the size of our family. Each time we had a baby, God provided a way of support. My logic struggled with the numbers, but by God's grace, we have been very blessed. This is true in any situation. I've learned we are rewarded for our faith, and there are blessings with obedience. They usually require lots of trust because some of our steps have looked absolutely crazy to those watching! But it's been worth every bit for my family.

*Dear Lord, thank you for your wisdom and protection and for leading me in all I do. Give me clarity, and help me make the right decisions. Go before me and prepare the way, so I can be in your will. Amen.*

# Day 12

*"Yes! Yahweh my healer has heard all my pleading and has taken hold of my prayers and answered them all."*
*- Psalms 6:9 TPT*

Do you ever think about what will actually happen after God answers your prayer? When something changes, we will have a new normal to walk out, which itself can be a refining process that puts us either on our knees or in the nut house. This is something I meditate on. I'm always asking the Lord for things, but not until recently have I realized that while He may answer, much is required from me to carry out His answer. It makes me think about my unanswered prayers. Some I am probably not ready to walk out. I have come to agree with what used to sound like a cliche: some of God's greatest gifts are unanswered prayers. I am thankful for God's timing.

*Lord, thank you for protecting me from what I thought I wanted and, instead, blessing me with what I didn't know I needed. I ask for peace and strength to press on when I'm told "no." Thank you for teaching me that a "no" is just a step to a better "YES." Amen.*

# Day 13

*"But they who wait for the Lord shall renew their strength; they shall mount up with wings like eagles; they shall run and not be weary; they shall walk and not faint."*
*- Isaiah 40:31 ESV*

This is one of my favorite promises from God. To wait on God means to hope expectantly in Him, trusting in His character and not our own strength. While waiting, He will give you new strength. He will empower you to withstand your situation and find victory through it. If we put our full faith and hope in the Lord, we will be transformed into His image. God will guide us on His path for our life, and there's nothing more amazing than that.

*Lord, I thank you that it's in waiting I can stop stressing and start believing God. It's in waiting I can stop complaining and start believing you are who you say you are, and you will do what you say you will do. Amen.*

# Day 14

*"Trust in the Lord with all your heart, and do not lean on your own understanding. In all your ways acknowledge him, and he will make straight your paths."*
- Proverbs 3:5-6 ESV

One of my deepest desires is to be in God's will. With so many voices vying for our allegiance, it's easy to get caught up in what the next step is and lose sight of where we've placed our trust. Will we trust in ourselves? In a government leader? In the latest trend? In popular opinion? In popular media channels? All of those things will eventually let us down or lead us astray—but not the Lord! His steps are sure, and His care is unmatched.

*Lord, I will trust you. I surrender my burdens to you. I trust the plan you have for my life and know it is better than my own. Give me peace and discernment to accept the things that are out of my control. I thank you for your continued wisdom and guidance in my life. Amen.*

# Day 15

*"In the same way, let your light shine before others, so that they may see your good works and give glory to your Father who is in heaven."*
- Matthew 5:16 ESV

I love that we don't have to chase what God wants to bring to us. We don't need to pursue goodness and mercy. Psalm 23 says it should follow us all the days of our lives. Psalm 40 tells us to be still and know He is God. We don't need to chase influence or pursue favor; we just need to arise and shine. Light doesn't need to strive—it just shines. When we radiate God as we were created to do, so much of what we chase will be magnetized in our direction.

His presence simply shining is more effective than our shouting. Influence and favor are the byproduct. Don't exhaust yourself today by chasing what God wants to bring to you. Let your light shine in darkness.

*Lord, I pray that the light of Christ in my heart may shine brightly before others in such a way that they may see the good works I do in your power and strength, and glorify you. AMEN.*

# Day 16

*"But he answered me, 'My grace is always more than enough for you, and my power finds its full expression through your weakness.' So I will celebrate my weaknesses, for when I'm weak I sense more deeply the mighty power of Christ living in me."*
– 2 Corinthians 12:9 TPT

I love this explanation of grace: "not only do we not get what we deserve, but also were given what we haven't earned." I don't know about you, but my life is filled with moments when I only survived because of God's grace.

The Japanese believe in a philosophy called Kintsukuori regarding things that are broken. For hundreds of years, they take a broken dish and, instead of discarding it, they glue it back together with silver or gold dust, highlighting the brokenness. Then that dish becomes useful again. And now it has a story. They celebrate the cracks and brokenness as part of the story of that object.

In the same way, God's grace works in us. We stand before Him with cracks in our hearts and our sinful ways, and He fills those cracks with the gold of grace. God accents our brokenness and makes us whole again. People with brokenness see the beauty of His grace and depth of it. I love how God can take our mess and make it our message!

*Holy Lord, I know I'm weak, but I also know you use my weakness to show your strength. God, give me the understanding that your grace is all I need, and that I can't earn it with my works alone. Help me be proud of my weaknesses, because they show your strength and protection. Amen.*

# Day 17

*"As iron sharpens iron, so a man sharpens the countenance of his friend."*
- Proverbs 27:17 NKJV

I sure appreciate the people in my life who tell it like it is. Real transformation only comes when truth is spoken. The only way for me to grow and sharpen is when my people tell me things I cannot see. I'm authentic, but it can be to a fault. Sometimes I'm too blunt, and while I see it's being authentic, I'm learning that I can say things on my heart—which may be confrontational—in a way that's gentle and kind. God's ways are higher than our ways, and we can elevate to be more like Him in our weaknesses when we listen to the sharpening words of a friend.

*Dear Lord, thank you for the relationships in my life. Place me in the path of wise people. Give me the wisdom to sharpen them. Give me humility so they can also sharpen me and make me better. Amen.*

# Day 18

*"I stand silently to listen for the one I love, waiting as long as it takes for the Lord to rescue me. For God alone has become my Savior. He alone is my safe place; his wraparound presence always protects me. For he is my champion defender; there's no risk of failure with God. So why would I let worry paralyze me, even when troubles multiply around me?"*
- Psalms 62:1-2 TPT

For many years, my soul did not rest. I was always looking to things of the world to fill the emptiness within me. When I finally surrendered to God at almost 30 years old, my soul found rest. No one knew better than me the turmoil I lived with before I met Jesus. I carried myself in such a way that the truth was hidden. But God knew I was nearly out of steam. He rescued me from the pit. Once I accepted the Lord as my savior, my eyes were opened to a whole new life, and I was able to see Him. I allowed Him to refine me continually into who He created me to be.

God is close to the broken-hearted, and He wants to rescue you. He sees your hurt, and He knows your pain. Remember, the God who created your heart is the same God who will heal it.

*Lord, you are my refuge and my strength. My soul finds rest in you alone. My hope comes from you. You are my rock and my salvation. I will not be shaken. Amen.*

# Day 19

*"Now all discipline seems to be painful at the time, yet later it will produce a transformation of character, bringing a harvest of righteousness and peace to those who yield to it."*
- Hebrews 12:11 TPT

While no one enjoys being disciplined, we want what discipline produces. It makes us better. Discipline helps us stay on a diet or complete a fitness program. If I don't discipline my kids, they will be unruly and lack character. In this same way, God demands discipline to shape us into His disciple. But let's be real: discipline is not fun. No one wants to be sent to the principal's office, put in jail, kicked off a team, or most of all, chastised by God. But it is discipline that brings righteousness and peace and makes us seek the Savior. We cannot do life without it.

*Dear Lord, help me relentlessly pursue the discipline of your Word. Give me a teachable spirit and a willingness to submit. No matter how difficult it is, strengthen me with the fruits of the spirit. Teach me to rely on and trust you as a child does a father. Amen.*

# Day 20

*"Therefore, confess your sins to one another and pray for one another, that you may be healed. The prayer of a righteous person has great power as it is working."*
*- James 5:16 ESV*

My deliverance came at a price—I had to allow what I'd been keeping in the dark for so long to come to light. I had to confess those things out of my mouth, so healing could happen. Can you imagine telling everyone you knew that you'd been lying to them for as long as you could remember? I lost some friends and gained some. It was a difficult time, but through that, God brought transformation.

Revealing your sin is the beginning of healing. But you must be aware of it and feel some regret in order to confess it. You don't have to admit your sin to everyone. But you need to admit it to someone. Life is so much better lived in freedom.

*Dear Lord, thank you for revealing your truth to my heart. Help me see my faults and quickly seek your forgiveness. When I confess my wrongdoing, help me avoid making the same mistakes again. I choose to obey your Word. Help me to pray for others and live in peace and unity to open the door for your healing. Amen.*

# Day 21

*"And the Word became flesh and dwelt among us, and we have seen his glory, glory as of the only Son from the Father, full of grace and truth."*
*- John 1:14 ESV*

I've gotten the qualities in this verse out of balance way too often. I tend to focus on the truth—the facts, the standards, and the gap between them (I struggle most with this in parenting). But without a doubt, it's grace that saved me. It's grace that softened my heart enough to be convicted. I was still confined to addiction when my family started going to church. The truth was I wasn't behaving rightly, but that didn't stop God's grace from delivering me and removing my desires for things not of Him. His act of grace set my family on a new journey. As I meditate on grace and truth, I see their need for balance. Truth without grace creates pretenders and hypocrites. But grace without truth creates a permissive version of faith that hurts everyone. Grace and truth together are a powerhouse! My goal is to lead with grace and proclaim the truth.

*Dear Lord, I give you all the glory. I know that your kindness leads to repentance. Your grace draws our hearts to you. I ask for an equal measure of grace and truth each day for me to be a powerhouse for your glory. Amen.*

# Day 22

*"Do not be anxious about anything, but in everything by prayer and supplication with thanksgiving let your requests be made known to God. And the peace of God, which surpasses all understanding, will guard your hearts and your minds in Christ Jesus."*
- Philippians 4:6-7 ESV

This verse says not to worry or be anxious about anything! Easier said than done, right? But I know this peace Paul refers to in this passage. This was the verse we hung on to during our season with Sage, when there was absolutely no reason to have peace. We had to learn how to take the first step, lay our problems at the feet of Jesus, and then trust His plans were good.

This doesn't mean we never worry. This verse reminds us when we do worry to turn back to prayer and praise. Knowing that the King of Kings cares about all the tiny details of our lives and has a plan gives us so much peace!

*Lord, thank you for being my ever-present help in my times of need. You know all things. It is you who numbers my days. My future is secure in you. Help me to turn my fears and worries into prayers and praise. As I turn to you and do this, I am confident I will be filled with the peace that only comes from you. In Jesus' name, Amen.*

# Day 23

*"Patient endurance is what you need now, so that you will continue to do God's will. Then you will receive all that he has promised."*
*- Hebrews 10:36 NLT*

Like me, you might find waiting hard. During the height of the COVID-19 pandemic, when Amazon's two-day shipping turned into two weeks, I found I no longer wanted the item once I had to wait. Delayed gratification is rare in our world, but it is still very real in our walk with God. This verse reminds me to be patient, to wait on the Lord, and to remember that none of this is for my glory. Only by trusting in Him and His will can I receive all He promised me. We can only go as fast as God wants us to go, no faster. I once heard a saying: God is never early or late, He is always right on time. A phrase we use in our home often is "His will; His way; my faith, no matter the cost."

You may be facing some difficulties in your life right now, but don't give up in doing God's will. Families all have problems. Money can be tight. Friendships change. Health fails. But the one constant you have is that God is always there. "Keep on keeping on."

*Dear God, I praise you for your strength and knowledge. I read over and over again in the Scriptures how you have strengthened, protected, and encouraged those who were feeling weak and vulnerable. I ask for your strength today, so that I may overcome temptation and accomplish good things, so that people may see and glorify you! I love you, Lord. Amen.*

# Day 24

> "The lovers of God who chase after righteousness will find all their dreams come true: an abundant life drenched with favor and a fountain that overflows with satisfaction."
> - Proverbs 21:21 TPT

Righteousness is the quality of being virtuous, honorable, or morally right. It's a direction we walk as we are empowered by the spirit of God in us and the righteousness of Christ that has been granted to us. We do not arch toward holiness apart from our grace-driven effort. We do not gravitate toward godliness, prayer, obedience to scripture, or faith and delight in the Lord on our own. We drift to compromise and call it tolerance. We drift to disobedience and call it freedom. We drift to superstition and call it faith. But this proverb says there a blessing in the pursuit of righteousness. We must be intentional. On the other side of righteousness are amazing things: life, prosperity, honor, eternal life.

*Dear Lord, you are worthy to receive glory and honor and power for you created all things. Direct my steps, show me the way and empower me to walk in it. Amen.*

# Day 25

*"Fear and intimidation is a trap that holds you back. But when you place your confidence in the Lord, you will be seated in the high place."*
– Proverbs 29:25 TPT

The fear of other's opinions is real. I've lived a huge part of my life in the comparison trap. I had to claw my way out of the valley of insecurities to get to the top of the mountain where my trust was solely in what God says about me. It is so freeing and peaceful. I wish it didn't take me over 40 years to conquer that mountain. The journey is not for the meek. While I lost a few things along the way, I gained so much more. God is in the business of freeing trapped people.

*Dear Lord, I place my trust in you alone. I ask that you drive away all fear of man and unproductive thoughts in my life, which hold me back from all you have for me. Amen.*

# Day 26

*"When the righteous cry for help, the Lord hears and delivers them out of all their troubles. The Lord is near to the brokenhearted and saves the crushed in spirit."*
*- Psalm 34:17-18 ESV*

What does it mean to be crushed in spirit? For me, it was finding out my teenager had an addiction to porn or had started cutting themselves. Unfortunately, I didn't allow God to be my refuge all those years ago. Instead, I was ruled by my own desires and pride, and because of that, our relationship suffered.

Many of the Psalms are laments—prayers that cry out in frustration, anger, and sorrow. God wants every part of us to be brought to Him. He knows the truth of our feelings regardless, but He draws more near to us when we intentionally lay it all at his feet. Psalmists often praised God by their weeping. Surrender all thoughts, even the ugly, to Him, and then praise His good and faithful love. He saves! He delivers!

*Lord, you are my refuge. There is no salvation or lasting comfort apart from you. You are the only one powerful enough to save and deliver me from my troubles. Help me lose my taste for pride, so I can taste and see the Lord is good. Amen.*

# Day 27

*"But the Helper, the Holy Spirit, whom the Father will send in my name, he will teach you all things and bring to your remembrance all that I have said to you."*
- John 14:26 ESV

Have you ever had those moments when you hear something on the radio, read something, or receive a random act of kindness and think, "I needed to hear, see, feel that?" I believe these moments are the Holy Spirit influencing us, moving us, nudging us. These are the moments I can sense something greater in and around me.

Jesus will never abandon us. He promises to send us the Holy Spirit to help us along the path, no matter the circumstances. Just think... God Himself will come live inside of us to comfort and help us through all life's challenges. We just have to invite Him in and allow Him to move.

*Holy Spirit, you are welcome to move in every part of my life. I acknowledge my need for you. I give you permission to have your way in my finances, in my dreams, my home, and the deepest parts of my heart and mind. Come like a flood into every corner of me—even the places I've kept hidden. You are my confidence. You are my source. Forgive me for looking to so many other sources for my confidence and security. I look to you, and you alone! Amen.*

# Day 28

*"Have I not commanded you? Be strong and courageous. Do not be frightened, and do not be dismayed, for the Lord your God is with you wherever you go."*
*- Joshua 1:9 ESV*

When we first learned how sick our unborn baby was at our 20-week ultrasound, our hearts were crushed. Multiple specialists advised us to terminate this pregnancy and start over. With so many "what ifs" looming, I struggled to find the strength to move forward. Once I came to the realization God was always with me, fear and worry dissipated, and I had the strength to keep moving.

In our own power, we naturally turn away and run from anything that brings emotional or physical pain. However, we can face those situations with confidence when we believe this verse. He will give you all the strength and courage you need to face whatever challenges come your way.

*Heavenly Father, I praise You that you have shown yourself faithful to your people, throughout all generations. Help me to rely on you in all the problems of life that I may face, knowing that you are with me wherever I go. In Jesus' name, AMEN.*

# Day 29

*"Rejoice always, pray without ceasing, give thanks in all circumstances; for this is the will of God in Christ Jesus for you."*
*- 1 Thessalonians 5:16-18 ESV*

So many things in life must be done repeatedly. Take dishes, for example. We wash our dishes, we dry them, we use them, and then after we use them, we do it all over again. Wash. Dry. Use. Repeat. Wash. Dry. Use. Repeat.

The same is true for our walk with the Lord. The Bible teaches us to be joyful, consistent in prayer, and thankful. In other words, "Rejoice. Pray. Give thanks. Repeat."

Joy comes from knowing we are never alone. Prayer is our ongoing conversation, Spirit to Spirit, child to father, human with God. Thanksgiving and joy are the great reminders that we have been blessed no matter what the outward circumstances imply.

So every moment of every day, those of us who follow Jesus Christ, who believe that He died for our sins and is the Lord of our lives, should remember to...

*Thank God every day that I pray,*
*Praise God for the day to-day,*
*I worship my Lord in Spirit and Truth,*
*Again thank You Lord I say.*

*Thank God every day for my time,*
*Praise God with my child like rhymes,*
*I worship You Lord with all of my heart,*
*Lord I thank You for all of the Signs.*
*Thank God every day for Your Son,*

*Praise God for His Holy One,*
*I worship my Lord by Reflecting His Love,*
*Thank the Lord till the day is done.*

*Thank God every night for the night,*
*Praise God for the blessing of Sight,*
*I worship You Lord in the darkest of times,*
*Thank You Lord for the Light of my life.*

Amen (author unknown)

# Day 30

*"And we know that for those who love God all things work together for good, for those who are called according to his purpose."*
– Romans 8:28 ESV

My life verse, and a promise for believers: those living for Christ, not those who claim to believe in God but are living like the devil. This verse says to those who love God and are doing their best to obey His commands, "Even though bad/sad/evil/wicked things will touch your life, I (God) will use them to ultimately bring about good, both in your life and in the world." He reigns. He is sovereign.

This has been true with every tragedy in my life. Although it was hard to see the silver lining when I miscarried a baby, or when I lost a baby after only three days of life, this verse gave me a comfort to hold on to. I have learned that God uses all the painful chapters, all the heartache, tears, disabilities, disadvantages, and disappointments for one purpose: to mold us into His likeness. I cling to the hope that not one thing happens in my life that the goodness of God will not one day transform into glory.

*Father, thank you that you work everything out for my good, even the things I don't see or understand. Give me eyes to see this at work in my life. You are the redeemer of all things. You exchange my brokenness for your glory and my good. Teach me and lead me as I submit to your authority. Give me your strength and peace today, and fill me with your faith to overcome. In Jesus' name, Amen.*

# About the Author

Misty Parenzan is a homeschool mom of nine, wife to the love of her life, and Mimi to two. She resides in the Florida Panhandle where she and her husband have built their lives over the last twenty years. Misty's love for the Lord wasn't built by her upbringing but rather by God's pursuit of her heart.

Misty walked out her convictions to stay home to mold her children's hearts to love God above all else and instill a love of learning. She encourages her kids to do hard things, love one another, put people before things, take risks, and have fun. When she is not reading books, playing outside, going to the beach, taking nature walks and bike rides, she is grocery shopping, paying bills, folding clothes, wiping tears and warming hearts. She enjoys her family and all things on land and sea. She has a gift of worship and songwriting. Misty is the friend you call when you need the unsweetened hard truth, sprinkled with grace. She means what she says and says what she means. "Author" is just another title to add to the culmination of experiences that make up her life, some of which you get to read and experience for yourself in *He Was Always There*. Who she is today and her zeal for the Lord are built on God's goodness and grace. She trusts without reservation that He works all things for His good.

For more information, visit www.hewasalwaysthere.com or scan the QR code.

# Endnotes

Wiersbe, W. W. (1996). *The Bible Exposition Commentary* (Vol. 2, p. 95). Wheaton, IL: Victor Books.

1. Elevation Worship. (2010). Give Me Faith. On *Kingdom Come.*
2. *Sallyclarkson.com.* SallyClarkson.com. (2012, November 8). Retrieved November 2022, from https://sallyclarkson.com/
3. Serenity Prayer attributed to Reinhold Neibuhr, 1892-1971)
4. Erickson, M. (2018, February 22). *Quotes and guidance from Billy Graham.* The Billy Graham Evangelistic Association of Canada. Retrieved November 2022, from https://www.billygraham.ca/stories/quotes-and-guidance-from-billy-graham/
5.

Made in United States
Orlando, FL
31 March 2023